CONCILIUM

Religion in the Eighties

CONCILIUM

David Tracy   Chicago, Ill.   U.S.A.
Knut Walf   Nijmegen   The Netherlands

General Secretariat: Prins Bernhardstraat 2, 6521 AB Nijmegen, The Netherlands

Concilium 185 (3/1986): Church Order

CONCILIUM

List of Members
Advisory Committee: Church Order

CANON LAW—
CHURCH REALITY

Edited by
James Provost
and
Knut Walf
English Language Editor
Marcus Lefébure

T. & T. CLARK LTD
Edinburgh

June 1986
T. & T. Clark Ltd, 59 George Street, Edinburgh EH2 2LQ
ISBN: 0 567 30065 X

ISSN: 0010-5236

Typeset by Print Origination Formby Liverpool
Printed by Page Brothers (Norwich) Ltd

Concilium: Published February, April, June, August, October, December.
Subscriptions 1986: UK: £19.95 (including postage and packing); USA: US$40.00
(including air mail postage and packing); Canada: Canadian $50.00 (including air mail
postage and packing); other countries: £19.95 (including postage and packing).

CONTENTS

Part III
Reception

EDITORIAL: CHURCH LAW—CHURCH REALITY

THE NEW Code of Canon Law has been in force in the Latin Church since 27 November 1983. It is law. Yet the time has jus begun in which the new code will be tested to see the extent to which it will mark the reality of Church life, including the legal realities which in fact take place in the Church. Will this code fulfill the expectations which preceded it? Will it provide for the months and years ahead a means for the Church to grow as a communion of faith, grace, charism and charity?[1] Ultimately, only time will tell. But we can already begin to explore the relationship of this new code to the reality of Church life as we know it. Moreover, such an effort is essential if the work of implementing this code is to be a reasoned, reflective effort which contributes to the self-building of the Church.

PRELIMINARY CONSIDERATIONS

Three factors deserve preliminary consideration. Law tends to be conservative; yet it also exercises a prophetic function. Church law, precisely as ecclesial, is a unique form of law.

(a). *Conservative.* One of the reasons for legislating is to conserve the values which have stood the test of time, and which the community desires to safeguard. This conservative role of law can enrich future generations by preserving for them the insight and wisdom of the past. But at the same time, law conserves the understanding of a value as it exists at the time the legislation is made.

Any law, including Church law, is marked by the values, concerns, debates and hopes of the moment in history when it is published. Yet the insights of one era, the concerns and debates of a particular moment in history, are not necessarily the same as those of succeeding generations. Moreover, the effort to legislate for a world-wide Church carries with it the special problems of relating to local churches and cultures which are at different stages in their history, at different degrees of development. Law, as it conserves values, expresses them in a culturally limited, dated fashion.

(b). *Prophetic.* Law also has a prophetic function. It teaches values. It can present ideals to which the community is called, challenges which stretch the community to grow. In this sense law is innovative, reaches to the future, calls forth the best in the community. But a prophet whose cry is not directed toward the realities in which he lives can be a rootless visionary; and prophets who speak only what is pleasing to the prince seldom produce true prophecy. So law, while challenging the community to greater fidelity, must be rooted in the life of the community and sensitive to its true needs; it must not fail to address important aspects of the community's life.

(c). *Ecclesial.* Church law has a unique ecclesial responsibility of conserving the pastoral wisdom and values already gained on the pilgrimage of God's people, and of facilitating in that community the work of the Spirit which dwells within the Christian faithful. This is an eminently pastoral, theological task. But it is also a particularly difficult one since the task is carried out in legal forms, indeed within the framework of a distinct legal system. When that legal system is foreign to the experience of a majority of the faithful, it may be more difficult to grasp in the law those perennial values which are to be made ever new in changing times and circumstances. *Church law and the reality of a world-wide Church are therefore in somewhat of a tension,* a tension further heightened by the rapid growth of the Church in the Third World and the pace of change within traditional Christian lands.

GENERAL OBSERVATIONS

In this issue of *Concilium* we turn to the new code to examine its relationship to the reality of the Church today, its fidelity to the Church's own self-understanding and its creativity in addressing the pastoral challenges of our times. Our authors have assessed the code from various perspectives.

Their careful evaluations have sought the benefit this code brings to the Church, but also the limitations which challenge us to critique the code in our fidelity to those principles[2] which inspired this revision of the Church's law.

Several common themes surface in the studies which compose this volume. While we must leave it to our readers to grasp those which are of special significance personally, it may be helpful to signal some of these themes which have a general interest: the meaning of the Church in the code; the respective roles of the hierarchy and of the Christian faithful in general; the application of the principle of subsidiarity; and ultimately, the relationship of law to Catholics' life of faith.

(a). *Ecclesiology*. Central to the code as an ecclesial document is its understanding of the Church. There were unresolved competing ecclesiologies at Vatican II which appear often in the same document. The same lack of consensus marks the ecclesiologies in the new code. Our authors identify *two main understandings of the Church* in the Code: *perfect society*, and *communion*. Various examples are given of each of these ecclesiologies in the code. They are placed in their historical context, and seen in light of the conciliar debates. But most significantly for our purposes, they imply distinct approaches to the making of law.

The perfect society theory provided one of the major foundations for the approach of the 1917 code. Imported from secular political theory, it originally was used to emphasise the independence and freedom of the Church when confronted with developing national States which sought to absorb all reality, including religion, within their sovereignty. Applied within the Church, the perfect society theory reduced ecclesial realities to secular paradigms, whether those of a monarchy or of democracy, and failed to grasp the unique nature of the Church. Yet this theory seemed especially suited to a Church which emphasised a clerical hierarchy and centralised control.

The communion ecclesiology which marks so many insights of Vatican II has a rich theological tradition of its own. The Church is a communion of the faithful, a hierarchical communion, a communion of churches. The implications for Church order reach into many aspects of the community's life.

To some extent the code presents these ecclesiologies simply put down side by side rather than integrated into a comprehensive vision. Four books of the code clearly draw on the 1917 code's perfect society understanding; two (Books III and IV) are more firmly based on the communion ecclesiology. Book II presents a special case, organised and in many sections based on a communion understanding of the Church, yet in other respects marking no change from the centralised and overly hierarchical emphasis of the previous code.

(b). *Hierarchy and people of God.* Can a code with such a split ecclesiology respond effectively to the expectations placed on it, and to the pastoral realities of the Church today? The answer is mixed. Several of our authors note the tension in the code in how canons deal with the role of the hierarchy and the responsibilities of all the people of God. The issue, however, is not one of monarchy or democracy. It is one of recognising the reality that the Church is the people of God, marked by the gifts of the Spirit, and served by those who are called from among their number in a special manner.

In some respects the code appears a continuation of a clerically dominated organisation, despite the growing acute shortage of clergy to staff such an organisation. Yet in other respects, practical opportunities are opened up for a broad participation by all the people of God in the mission of the Church and in serving its communion. These mixed results are ambiguous, a further indication that the implementation of the code will be even more significant than the process of its drafting and promulgation.

(c). *Subsidiarity.* The principle of subsidiarity is noted in many of these studies as critical in the formulation of the law, and even more crucial in its application in practice. Various institutes are studied which provide for subsidiary function, whether within parishes and dioceses, in the workings of conferences of bishops, in adaptation to rural and missionary settings, in the life of religious institutes, or in the relationship of ritual churches *sui iuris.*

Yet there remains a tension between control by the central authorities of the Church universal, the proper responsibilities and prerogatives of ritual churches *sui iuris*, and the appropriate powers of diocesan bishops and conferences of bishops. Such tension can be creative or it can weaken the Church's life; the opportunities the new code presents here will clearly require serious effort.

(d). *Law and the life of faith.* Ultimately the new code will be judged on how well it serves the reality of the community's life in faith. Here again the responses of our authors are mixed. The new code does reflect a major effort to respond to the faith needs of parishes. It is more sensitive to the charism of religious. It seeks to provide a more equitable place for women in the faith community.

But at the same time, major concerns are expressed for how realistically the code relates to certain key areas of Catholic belief and practice. The treatment of marriage, particularly the religious question of faith and marriage in Western and Third World cultures, leaves much to be desired. The understanding of penalties evidences some attempt at a more religiously based approach, but winds up falling back on a secular concept divorced from the faith reality of Church.

From a different perspective, the new code is seen as being simply out of touch with major segments of the Catholic experience, primarily that of the Third World. With over half the Catholics now living in Third World countries, and the proportion increasing every year, the inability of a primarily European approach to relate effectively to the religious reality of such a major portion of the Church is indeed regrettable. However, as our authors intimate, the problem is larger than that of the code itself and presents an historic challenge to world-wide Catholicism which will take more than lawyers to address.

THE ARTICLES

E. Corecco provides an important theological perspective for considering the new code. He identifies the two ecclesiologies present in the canons— perfect society and communion—and develops examples of each. Despite several regrettable weaknesses in applying the communion ecclesiology, he is able to point to the important communions of the faithful, of churches, and of ministers which mark the basic framework of the law.

R. Potz sets the new code in the context of legal theories today, particularly the historicity of law. This codification is one moment in an on-going historical process. The tension between perfect society and communion ecclesiologies is further demonstrated in his analyses of the seven books of the new code, and in relationship to specific topics in the law.

The setting of the new code within the communion of local churches is detailed by *P. Husizing*. Drawing on the teachings of the Second Vatican Council, he provides a careful analysis of the one Church existing in each local church, and of the one Church existing from and out of the local churches. His study is an important reminder that the proper interpretation of the code requires continued study of Vatican II.

An overall evaluation in light of the expectations which preceded the code is provided by *F. Morrisey*. The new code generally lives up to the various criteria presented for it in advance. The author is able to identify several significant positive elements in the law. Nevertheless, a number of points remain which require adaptation or substantial change in the years ahead.

Turning to specific areas of pastoral concern, the next set of studies explore the code from within. They examine the revised law in terms of how it relates to the reality of Catholic life today.

J. Bernard places the law on marriage in the context of the major cultural shifts taking place in Western societies today. He finds the code taking a prophetic stance against the prevailing privatisation of marriage and calling for a commitment of the community to aid the couple. But he also finds the new law out of touch with the very real pastoral problems of faith commitment on the part of those who enter marriage today.

In preparing the new code serious questions were raised about the theological rationale for penalties in the Church. *L. Gerosa* explores these issues, and the manner in which the new code addresses or fails to address them. He, too, finds a double spirit in the code: a theological sensitivity to communion, which provides a significant advance in the understanding of penalties in comparison to the former code; and a positivistic approach which merely repeats the old code's presumptions without making them more intelligible to people today.

The treatment of parish life fares better, in the view of *J. Huels*. The code's new approach gives priority to the parish community, providing for a variety of participative structures and ministries. Problem areas remain, however, ranging from shortcomings in the code's treatment of certain topics to the wider issues of the complexity of Church law affecting parish practice and the growing shortage of priests.

E. McDonough values the enhanced juridic condition of women in the new code and details how this has been achieved in considering women as laity, and in viewing women in contrast to men. Some legal problems remain, as well as the broader issues of clergy-laity relations and the loss to the Church of the ability, competence and experience of many of its members by the exclusion of women from positions restricted to clergy.

R. Hill finds the section on religious in the new code to be one of the most thoroughly reworked. His analysis of four essential elements in religious life points to the diversity in practice as it is found in North America. Beneath this diversity is the ongoing tension over the value of personal freedom and integrity in contrast to the limits placed by tradition and law.

The four concluding studies in this volume approach the new code from a variety of experiences. These are illustrative of the various contexts in which a world-wide Church functions, and therefore in which its law must be considered.

The relationship of the new Latin Church code to Eastern Catholic Churches is analysed by *J. Faris*. In the context of a Church which is in reality a communion of ritual churches *sui iuris*, the provisions of the new code touch on Church membership, sacramental law and practice, and key structures of Church organisation. The juridic ordering of the whole Church will not be complete until the revision of the Eastern Churches' law is completed.

A. Stein provides an illuminating review of the reaction to the new Roman Catholic code of law from within the German speaking churches issuing from the Reform. Positive elements are identified as well as concerns relating to the role of the papacy, the status of the laity, and sacramental law. Yet the code does provide a certain clarity which is important for the ecumenical dialogue.

The new code has been promulgated for a world-wide Church. To what extent it relates to the reality of Church life in Africa is the concern of *S. Bwana*. He finds the law, as indeed much of traditional Catholic practice, still foreign to local cultures. This can be problematic when applied to such realities as marriage, which affect the very living of faith in divers cultural settings. Although the code is designed for the normative authority of the Roman Pontiff over the whole Church, instruments of adaptation are needed to adjust its provisions to local life; one such instrument is the church tribunal.

J. Dammert-Bellindo writes from the perspective of a bishop in a rural diocese of the Peruvian Andes. He finds many positive elements in the new code at the practical level. Yet it remains very European, and very urban. From the point of view of Church life in his and other rural dioceses, it presents a diocesan organisation which is too complex and detailed and fails to relate effectively to a Church becoming more and more dependent on service by the laity.

A CODE IN THE REALITY OF CHURCH TODAY

What can we conclude from these analyses? Admittedly they are only a beginning. The code and its application in the life of the Church will be an object of study and reflection for years to come. But already we can discern certain lines of force which bear considering in the years ahead.

First, the code exists. It will be put to many uses in many different settings. It has already made itself felt in the actions of conferences of bishops, diocesan churches, the life of parishes and associations. It is itself a reality, a text which has taken on an existence of its own which becomes increasingly distant from the process by which the code was formed.

Second, there are ambiguities in this code. Some of these are quite fundamental, such as the very meaning of Church which underlies the new law. These ambiguities are not unlike, and indeed are related to, those ambiguities which marked the council. They will continue to provide the opportunity for various uses to be made ot the same texts.

Third, the code presents the Church with important opportunities. Over the short term, there is the challenge to take full advantage of the subsidiarity, flexibility and options which are present in the new law. In this way a more creative application of Catholic practice can be made within various cultures. The communion of the Church can be strengthened and its mission carried out more effectively in the divers circumstances of the world today.

Over the long term, there are important challenges to the continued work of scholars and researchers. As a product of a given moment in time, strongly influenced by a particular legal culture, the 1983 code is already dated. These studies have begun the difficult but essential task of identifying points to be addressed in the ongoing process of legal reform in the Church.

Fourth, there is a special temptation against which we must steel ourselves. It is the temptation to become so fascinated with the new code that it seduces the Catholic community, or at least its scholars and leaders, into a new juridicism. John Paul II continues to call for the council to be the interpreter of the code, rather than vice-versa. Yet in practice appeals are increasingly made to the code rather than to conciliar documents, and the perspective of the code begins to dominate the reactions of pastors and bishops. Fascination with the law can obscure a clear vision of the reality of Church life.

The purpose for the code is not to replace the gospel, nor to insulate us from the realities in which the Church lives nor even to supplant the *magisterium's* formal pronouncements at Vatican II. Rather, it is to provide a means of applying the Gospel and *magisterium* to the reality of Church life: To return to the central point of John Paul II in promulgating this code, its purpose is to facilitate grace, faith, charism and charity in the life of the community and in the individuals who make up that community.

The law by itself will never be able to achieve this end. The life of faith, the reality of grace and charism, the bonding force of charity are realities which reside in the spirits of people, not in the words of a lawbook. To achieve the purpose of the law is a truly human endeavour, an eminently Christian one. As many of our authors caution, it is the implementation of the law by persons which holds the key to the effective application of the code to Church reality.

James Provost
Knut Walf

Notes
    1. John Paul II identified the purpose of law as facilitating these values in the life of

both the ecclesial society and the individuals who belong to it. See apostolic constitution *Sacrae disciplinae leges*, 25 January 1983: *AAS* 75/2 (1983) xi.

2. These principles are repeated in the Preface to the code, a clear indication they remain valid as instruments for interpretation of the new law. See *Prefatio*, *AAS* 75/2 (1983) xxi-xxii.

PART I

General

Eugenio Corecco

Ecclesiological Bases of the Code

1. THE ECCLESIOLOGY OF 'SOCIETA'S'

THE NEW Code of Canon Law contains *two ecclesiologies*, which can be defined as being of '*societas*' and of '*communio*'[1], which the consistent lines taken by its authors, faithful to the principle of abstract codification, manifest in all their unbridgeable separateness.

(a) The very concept of codification stems from the ecclesiology of *societas*.[2] Although codifications have taken different forms at different periods in history, there is no escaping the fact that doctrinally and methodologically they refer to a gnoseological experience—that of illuminism—posited as a purely rational alternative to Christian theological culture.[3] The ecclesiology of society, through the *Ius Publicum Ecclesiasticum* (IPE), claims to demonstrate that the Church, even as '*mysterium salutis*', takes on, both *ad intra* and *ad extra*, the same juridical and institutional aspects as any other perfect society, and in doing so inevitably ploughs canonical order into the soil of an almost atavistic 'institutional hegemony'[4], demanded by a secular notion of law, which exalts the concept of competence above the more ecclesiological one of participation.[5]

Furthermore, this approach values, pragmatically and almost con-naturally, derived *institutional features* (pope-college-universal church, bishop-priest-local church relationships, ecumenical and local councils, parishes, etc.) at the expense of primarily constitutive features (sacrament, Word, charism . . .) thereby avoiding giving any ultimate rationale to juridical structures.[6] It should not, therefore, be surprising that this 'societal' ecclesiology, still overshadowed as it is by the notion of the '*societas perfecta*', provides the *infrastructure of the four books* (I, V, VI and VII) in which the Code of 1917 still survives substantially intact.

(b) In Book I, the adoption of the technique of 'general norms', an expression typical of modern codifications, has led to the application of strictly legal rules to its contents, even where these are theological. For example: (i) The faithful, though singled out in Book II as the principal subject of canonical order, are not defined on the basis of their ecclesiological identity, but with the romanising category of 'physical persons', deviating from their theological profile even in the understanding of meaning of the term 'moral person'. In fact, the element that distinguishes the faithful from the moral person is not that of his natural physicality, but that of his sacramental status. In effect, the faithful does not pre-exist the Church, as the human person does the State, and the moral person (though distinguished from the juridical person in canons 113 and 114) cannot be an ecclesiological holder of *sacra potestas*. Neither the Catholic Church, nor the Holy See (nor the College of Bishops), exercise their *potestas* by virtue of the fact that they can conventionally be defined as moral persons which is furthermore a concept alien to divine lae.

(ii) Connected with the notions of physical person and moral (and juridical) person are juridical actions and the distinction between public and private actions. The societal approach leaves out of account the fact that the most basic juridical acts, ecclesiologically speaking, are the sacraments, whose binding juridical power is soteriological rather than social, and so goes on to restate norms about their validity which are largely inapplicable to the sacraments (canons 113 and 114). The distinction between public and private, applied to associations, relegates the greater part of these to a virtually para-ecclesial sphere of existence. In State affairs it is possible to distinguish between society and the public organisation of power, i.e. the State. In Church affairs, however, the faithful as an association cannot be downgraded to the realm of the 'private'. As holders of the common priesthood and of the *sensus fidelium*, they make up the first and irreplaceable pole of the institution of the Church. The other pole of this institution, the ministerial priesthood, cannot claim, as the State can, the exclusive function of representing the ecclesial institution.

(iii) Another central institution that suffers a marked theological reduction in a societal conception of the Church is that of *'potestas regiminis, seu iurisdictionis'*. The fact that the conciliar notion of *'potestas sacra'* has disappeared from the Code is already highly significant. Treated outside the ecclesiological context of the power of order and *sacra potestas*, the *'potestas regiminis' appears to derive from the societal structure of the Church, rather than from the specific nature of a communio*, which cannot be reduced to a human society 'raised' to a supernatural level. Rather than taking on the aspect of a saving power, whose binding force derives from Word and Sacrament, it assumes a physiological make-up similar to that of State power. Despite the solid support for the organisational implications of the separation of powers (can. 135), stemming from the Synod of 1967[7], the new Code still places the power of jurisdiction (can. 129ff) after the norms it establishes concerning laws (can. 7ff) and administrative actions (can. 29ff), even though these are only functions of the *potestas regiminis*. In this, the Code remains faithful to the systematic principle of the voluntarist tradition, in accordance with Suarez's *De Legibus*, which antedates Montesquieux. This positivist approach, in the rulings on laws, customs and administrative acts (as indeed on juridical functions in Book VII), conserves the same earlier juridical-technical connotation, shorn of any ecclesiological evaluation. The norms guiding laws still have no reference to the *sensus fidei* of the faithful, as if the juridical function were an exclusive possession of the hierarchy. The partici-pation of all the faithful (somewhat recovered in Book II through their presence in synodal structures, and in other Books), is reduced in this context to recognition of the active subjectivity of the '*communitas fidelium*' (can. 23) formed by custom and, very indirectly, to interpretation of the law through custom, '*optima legum interpres*' (can. 27).

In the field of administrative function, structured with the same rigorously juridical criteria as legislative function, there is nevertheless a substantial ecclesiological gain in Book I itself. This is that the criterion whereby dispensation from a law can only be given by the author of that law has been replaced by the criterion that the diocesan bishop by virtue of his office itself, possesses all the faculties necessary for the wellbeing of his faithful (can. 87).

(c) The societal approach surfaces again in the way in which the Code conceives the exercise of *potestas regiminis* in the *sacramental and extra-sacramental fields*. In the first, the power of jurisdiction, which terminologi-cally assumes the guise of a simple 'faculty' devoid of its own content, intervenes in an extrinsic manner, in regard to the power of order, in producing the sacramental effect (penance, can. 966ff; confirmation, can. 882ff; matrimony, can. 1111, 2; sacramentals, can. 1168). In the extra-sacramental field, where it takes on the guise of a true and proper *potestas*, it is considered a power with its own material content, different from the power of order: thus in dispensations (from vows, can. 1196; from oaths, can. 1203; from matrimonial impediments, can. 1079, 2-4; in remission of penances *in foro externo* (can. 1354ff); and in granting of indulgences (can. 955). This double dualism, in the rigid separation of order from jurisdiction, as though they were *two different powers instead of two purely formal functions of the one sacra potestas*, and in the different causal role attributed to jurisdiction in sacramental and extra-sacramental fields, is already contained '*in nuce*' in canon 131 in which, in the wake of the 1967 Synod, it is still established that the power of jurisdiction should operate *in foro interno* only in an exceptional way.

(d) The same societal inspiration governs the ground plan of Book VII. Typically canonical procedures for the canonisation of saints and teaching the faithful are upheld in the new Code. Those concerning the constitutional status of the faithful (marriage, orders, belonging to the *communio*, that is, 'penal' processes), are, however, relegated, by virtue of purely juridical theoretical presuppositions, to simple 'special' procedures grafted on to the ordinary courts, despite the fact that these, through their affinity to civil courts, are judged in canon 1446 to be supplementary procedures. Canon 1446's indication that trials are to be avoided by resolving disputes when no great legal issues are involved shows traces of the ecclesiology of communion, even though insufficiently to overturn the general thrust of Book VII. In fact, it is only within the confines of the modern State system that judicial procedures exist as institutional projections essential to and constitutive of the very being of judicial power, which is autonomous and separate from other arms of authority. In canonical ordering the existence of the judicial function doesn't depend on the existence of procedures. *Potestas sacra*, as the power of loosing and binding, can operate even outside procedures. These, as historically unrenounceable and definitively imposed, for the sake of greater juridical certainty and equality before the law (generally non-absolute socio-juridical principles), remain superstructures added on to the *potestas sacra*.

(e) In Book V too, the overall juridical plan remains within the parameters of the IPE. The key to the whole system is found in canons 1245, 1 and 1260, with their peremptory confirmation of the Church's right to possess inherited goods, independent of the civil power, or its right to require from the faithful the financial contributions needed to carry out its purposes. In the duty of the faithful to contribute to the needs of the Church (canons 222, 1 and 1262), there is not the merest hint that they might also, in however small a measure, be called on *also to practice communion on the level of material goods*. This idea does emerge, however, though implicitly and without affecting the legislative basis, in the redefinition of the purposes of the Church's possessions (can. 1242, 2), thanks to the greater attention paid there to the earliest tradition, in which the connection with the eucharistic community was clear, and in the recognition of conciliar institutes in canon 1274, which defines the structure of the presbyterate as a communion. So the Church overall continues to appear hypostasized in the hierarchy, which, like the State, sets itself in a relationship of otherness to the faithful, responsible for carrying out by itself, on the basis of semi-inquisitorial considerations, tasks which the faithful have to acquiesce in without being truly protagonists of them.[8]

(f) The juridical-formal framework of Book VI also reflects that of modern codes of criminal law. *Its whole theoretical and epistemological thrust is not towards communio*, to which *excomunicatio* is related, *but to natural law principles of restoration* (can. 1341) *and of the power of coercion* (can. 1311). This, despite the fact that excommunication cannot theoretically be included under the notion of punishment, which belongs to the general theory of law.[9] This fact undermines the whole theoretical and epistemological construct of the Book, with its expansive treatment of other minor sanctions. The very preferential option for *ferendae* sentences rather than *latae sententiae* is not based on the logic of *communio* (allowing authorities to approach faithful in difficulties in a more personal way), but, as the 1967 Synod explicitly suggested, on that of bringing about a vision of a *societas perfecta* that is more in keeping with the sensibilities of modern juridical thinking. But in this Book too, in canon 1341, there is a hint of the ecclesiology of *communio*; this canon confers, despite its marginal systematic placing, supplementary status on the whole sanctions apparatus. This canon, like those dealing with imputability (1312-30) and on the specific application of punishments (1345-63), together with the general principle underlying canon 1339 and the nature of excommunication, voids the whole argument of Book VI of any real and specific content, creating an unbridgeable gap between its material and formal content.

2. THE ECCLESIOLOGY OF *COMMUNIO*

The essence of the principle of *communio* consists in the fact of postulating the *total immanence, and the inseparability, of all the elements that make up the Church*. This is seen, for example, in the structural relationship of *reciprocity* between Sacrament and Word, between the common and the ministerial priesthood, between the faithful and the Church, between duties and rights, between universal and local Church, between the pope and the college of bishops, between the bishop and his priests. This ecclesiology, which underlies Books II, III and IV of the new Code, is not always expressed with the coherence one would like.

(a) The *basic obstacle* to its expression is the fact that the Code displays an ecclesiological approach suffering from an *excess of pragmatism*. This stems from several causes:

(i) The first of these is its adoption of the ecclesiological principle '*Sacramenta (et Verbum) ab Ecclesia*' instead of the principle '*Ecclesia a Sacramentis (et Verbo)*'.[10] Word and Sacrament thereby become elements that derive from, instead of being generative of, the Constitution of the Church, the nucleus of which, according to the intention of the Code at least, is contained in its Book II on 'The People of God'. The sacrament of baptism alone, in canons 96 and 204, is placed as an element that generates a specific and corresponding set of rules: those dealing with the physical person, and those dealing with the rights and duties of the faithful. The rules for clerics, on the other hand, are divorced from the context of orders, just as those on sanctions are taken out of the sacramental context of penitence; the norms concerning the universal and the local Church have no immediate connection the Eucharist, and the family does not appear as the social embodiment of the sacrament of matrimony. The canons on the Eucharist and penance are rich in definitions with ecclesiological resonances, but these are still not sufficient to prevent the sacraments being treated as they were in the Code of 1917, *from a functional rather than constitutive standpoint.*

(ii) This approach is also responsible for the *minimal utilisation of the sensus fidei of the faithful* (taken up in canon 750 in a seriously mutilated form *when compared to Lumen gentium* 12, 1) and of the *common priesthood* (can. 836).[11] These concepts exercise absolutely no influence on the overall systematic organisation of the legislative material. If the Code had dug to the very depths of ecclesiology and defined the faithful primarily as titular subjects of the common priesthood and the *sensus fidei*, it would have been able to bring out, in a systematic way, the *structural immanence* of all the *faithful both in Sacrament and Word*, and in the sacred ministries, showing that the formal distinction between order and jurisdiction, in which their *potestas sacra* is situated, has its roots in their various forms of participation in the same Sacrament and the same Word, which affect the whole of the faithful.

(iii) A further obstacle to a full exposition of the ecclesiology of *communio* was the adoption by the three central Books of the arguments of *Lumen gentium* concerning the participation of the whole People of God in the '*tria munera*' of Christ. The inadequacy of this for grasping the mystery of the Church is shown by the fact that the new Code is unable to find theoretical and scientific arguments   to develop the practical consequences of the *munus regendi*. This leads to an opposition between the People of God and one of their functions and a subtle process of '*reductio ad unum*' of the '*munus regendi*' of the laity into that of the hierarchy.

(iv) Another obstacle, which can be attributed either to Vatican II or to contemporary ecclesiology, standing in the way of a fully developed exposition of the communal principle of immanence, is the fact that *the universal Church and the local Church* are unconsciously treated as though they were two materially separate entities, and therefore potentially in competition with each other, rather than *two merely formally distinct dimensions of the one Church of Christ*, set out in all its uniqueness in the central norms of canons 96 and 369. The principle of immanence in both universal and local Church is clearly stated in the formula '*in quibus et ex quibus*' in canon 368—so much so that it can be considered as an ontological and gnoseological paradigm of the very structure of *communio*. But if this principle had been placed at the beginning of Part II of Book II and referred directly to the Church of Christ, it would have had a stronger and wider influence on the whole of the Code.

(v) A further consequence of the pragmatic and institutional approach in the legislative content of the Code is the *obliteration of charism*, as though this were not an essential element in the Constitution of the Church.[12] The faithful are definable not only through the sacramentality of their being and lives, but also through the possibility of their becoming the rightful subjects of charisms. Without this potential charismatic dimension the faithful and, consequently, the People of God, are prevented from reaching the fulness of their true identity in the Church and its juridical structures. There are certain references to the action of the Holy Spirit, which nevertheless do not necessarily coincide with the specific action of charism (as, for example, in canons 369, 375, 1, 573, 1, 747, 1 and 879), to the gifts of the Spirit (can. 577 and 605). Yet the Code, giving in to the recurrent objection that charism is not a juridical fact, has not gone to the heart of the constitutional structure of the Church. *Charism does not exist autonomously*. It is *always* conferred on the two basic elements that make up the institution of the Church: the common priesthood (with its *sesus fidei*) and the ministerial priesthood. While by definition not belonging to the sphere of juridical reality and institution, it does belong to the Constitution of the Church and has a very precise juridical validity, either because it should underlie the judgements of pastors, or because, along with baptism, charismatic gifts serve as the basis of the rights and duties of the faithful in their work of spreading the gospel (*Ad Gentes* 28, 1). The Spirit is not to be extinguished (LG 12, 3), but sets (like rights and duties) non-transgressible limits to the exercise of *sacra potestas*. Unlike what happens in the sphere of public organisation of State power, the institution of the Church is not the same thing as its Constitution, but only one element of it. The inseparability and mutual immanence of institution and charism are a further specific implication of the principle of *communio*. It is only on the basis of an ideological misunderstanding that their relationship has been seen as one of opposition; this derives from a *supposed opposition between charity and the law*.

(vi) A final aspect of the pragmatic approach to ecclesiology is *the elimination* from canon 205 *of the conciliar phrase 'possessing the Spirit of Christ'* (LG 14, 2). The reduction of the criteria for accepting the faithful as 'fully incorporated' into the Church to the three classic elements in Bellarmine's definition shows a conception in which grace is not considered as an element necessarily immanent in the institution. That grace, like charism, possesses an independent juridical value, regardless of where it surfaces (as with the '*tria vincula*') or, to a lesser extent, through recognisable institutional aspects, is clear from canon 916. Non-possession of grace affects incorporation into full communion and the exercise of the rights of the faithful.

(b) Despite these limitations, the ecclesiology of *communio lies at the roots of all three levels on which the Church exists*: the '*communio fidelium, Ecclesiarum et ministeriorum*'.[13] On the level of *communio Ecclesiarum*, it is recognised that the immanence of the universal and local dimension of the one Church of Christ is unhesitatingly affirmed in the formula '*in quibus et ex quibus*' in canon 368. The universal Church, made up of all the local Churches, is realised in each local Church. This means that all local Churches are ontologically immanent in each local Church. *Communio*, therefore, does not arise only from the constitutive and hierarchical relationship of each local Church to the Roman Church (e.g. canons 331, 349, 3), but also from the reciprocal relationship between individual local Churches. Though this derives from the first, it is no less essential for understanding the *communio Ecclesiarum*, the ontological and gnoseological basis of the *communio ministeriorum*, which binds bishops, priests and perhaps even deacons together reciprocally and specifically. Following Vatican II the Code expresses the specific nature of the *communio ministeriorum* in the term '*communio hierarchica*' (canons 336, 375, 2; PO 15, 2), which is really a broader term, since all levels of *communio* are included in the hierarchical dimension (can. 212, 1).

On the level of *communio fidelium* it is worth analysing the emergence of the ecclesiology of communion in more detail. Canon 209, 1 shows that communion invests the ontological structure of the faithful, delineating their anthropological and ecclesial identity. Effectively, the duties and rights of living in communion with God and the Church form the ontological basis and immanent logic of a series of duties and rights, derived not from natural law but from divine law, such as those formulated in canons 209, 2, 210, 211, which in turn become the starting points for other cases which build up the juridical heritage of the faithful (e.g. canons 212-3, 215, 217).

(i) The principle of immanence in *communio* surfaces in other aspects of the question. The new Code, distancing itself from the LEF (*Lex ecclesiae fundamentalis*) (in accordance with the tendencies of modern constitutionalism), does not attribute the constitutional qualification of 'fundamentality' to the duties and rights of the faithful and the laity, which are divided into their respective categories. This brings about a structural conflict situation (given that this is possible and exists) in the relationship between faithful and hierarchy, which is nevertheless subordinate to the citizen-State relationship, determined as this is by the pre-existence of the human subject and by the need to guarantee a sphere of autonomy to the individual. Since the duties and rights of the faithful are, on the other hand, conferred by the Church (or recognised in order when they originate in natural law), through the sacraments, the concept of autonomy cannot be applied to the juridical situation of the faithful on the same theoretical bases. Both faithful and hierarchy, in effect, belong to the institution of the Church, which means that the realtionship is not set up between person and institution, but between person and person.

· (ii) The second aspect consists in the fact that the system employed by the Code gives ontological preference to the notion of duty over that of right. In effect, almost half the cases catalogued, stated as rights, are in fact derivations of duties. It is symptomatic that wherever the Code introduces cases drawn more or less directly from natural law (e.g. canons 218–222, 2, 231, 2), the notion of right prevails over that of duty. The result is that in these cases right can be transferred to third parties (hierarchy), while the duties deriving from *ius divinum* remain inherent in first parties and are transferable only in so far as they become rights. This priority of duty is not philosophical-voluntarist in origin, but ecclesiological. It stems from the dependence of all the faithful on Christ who calls them to communion with the Father and the Church, as canon 209, 1 affirms.

(iii) The third aspect of the *communio fidelium* lies in the fact that the faithful do not exist as such, but as an ecclesiological reality immanent in all the other states in which the faithful live their lives. This immanence is assured by the principle of equality proclaimed in canon 208. This creates *a deep and reciprocal immanence of the three states*, which cannot be reduced to superstructures inherited from the Middle Ages, since they are brought about by the sacraments (of baptism and order) or by charism (the evangelical counsels). The status of the evangelical counsels is not simply set above the other two, as a wrong reading of canon 207, 1 might suggest; it has its own constitutional priority: that of making prophecy present, just as the lay state has its priority in the field of secular responsibility and the clerical state has its responsibility for the unity of the '*communio Ecclesiae et Ecclesiarum*'.[14]

(iv) In the course of its central evaluation of faith, the new Code has also revalued the laity, both in its methodology—considering them before the clergy—and in its substance (though not without gaps)—concerning their participation in all three *munera*, to the point where they can hardly be distinguished from deacons. A more decisive evaluation of their '*Indolis saecularis*' (a concilar concept not taken up in the Code), which emerges only in four norms (or groups of norms: canons 225, 2, 227, 237, 226, 793, 796–9), would have avoided the dualistic error of suggesting that the secular responsibility which is the special province of the laity is expressed as such solely in their encounter with the world and not also in their internal encounters with Church structures. Only this double application enables the laity to be the point of contact between Church and world and the point of immanence between the economy of redemption and that of creation, two economies which are found indissolubly immanent in the sacrament of matrimony, which is precisely the highest expression of secularity. The prevalence of the sacramental definition of the laity in the new Code (v. LG 31, 1), contrary to the overall emphasis in the conciliar texts, over a definition that lays greater stress on their secularity, leads to an overall clericalised picture of the laity.

Translated by Paul Burns

Notes

1. See A. Acerbi *Due ecclesiologie; ecclesiologia giuridica e ecclesiologia di comunione nella 'Lumen Gentium'* (Bologna 1975).

2. For the works of the writer on the new Code, see the articles mentioned in the biographical note.

3. For the canonical understanding of law, see E. Corecco '"*ordinatio rationis*" o "*ordinatio fidei*"? Appunti sulla definizione della lege canonica' in *Communio* 36 (1977) 48–69 (Ital.); 3 (1978) 22–39 (Fr.).

4. See R. Sobánski 'Rechtstheologische Vorüberlegungen zum neuen kirchlichen Gesetzbuch' in *Theol. Quart.* 163 (1983) 178–88.

5. See G. Alberigo 'Egemonia dell'institucione nella cristianità?' in *Cristianesimo nella storia* 5 (1984) 49–68.

6. See G. Colombo 'La teologia della Chiesa particolare' in *La Chiesa locale* ed. A. Tessarolo (Bologna 1970) pp. 17–38.

7. The ten principles laid down by the 1967 Synod for the revision of the Code, read 20 years later, reveal a very serious ecclesiological deficiency, despite their apparent modernity.

8. See E. Corecco 'La Sortie de l'Eglise pour raison fiscale: Le problème canonique' in *Sortir de l'Eglise* (Fribourg 1982) pp. 11–67.

9. On this point, see the article by L. Gerosa in this issue.

10. It would be enough to substitute the title of Books III and IV with '*De verbo Dei*' and '*De sacramentis*' for this ecclesiological plan to appear in all its clarity.

11. See E. Corecco 'Riflessione giuridico-istituzionale su sacerdozio comune e sacerdozio ministeriale' in *Popolo de Dio e Sacerdozio* (Padua 1983) pp. 80–129.

12. See J. Komonchak 'The Status of the Faithful in the new Code' in *Concilium* 147 (7/1981) 37–44.

13. On these three levels of *communio*, see W. Aymans 'Einführung in das neue Gezetsbuch der lateinischen Kirche' in *Arbeitshilfen no. 31* of the Secretariat of the German bishops' conference (Bonn 1983).

14. On the 'circular' relationship of the three states of life, see H. Urs von Balthsasar *Christlicher Stand* (Einsiedeln 1977), esp. pp. 294–314.

Richard Potz

The Concept and Development of Law According to the 1983 CIC

AWARENESS THAT *law is subject to history* is one of the few generally accepted principles of jurisprudence. This also applies to law in the Church, which is both a visible assembly and a spiritual communion, combined in a unique and complex reality composed of human and divine elements.

Canon law also has a *foundation in ecclesiology*, but that does not mean that the history of law in the Church is a one-way street, along a path indicated by salvation-history, leading to ever more perfect law; it is a history of success and failure in the attempt to establish practical justice in the light of Christ's saving act.

Yet this in no way implies a relativism; it means that in the history of canon law, as in other fields, we can detect many overlapping, complementary, and sometimes contradictory processes. As well as elements that are originally given and thus unalterable, and the results of irreversible processes, there are also cyclic factors. Among the latter is the development of law, the thrust of which is largely influenced by the relationship of tension between the stability of law and the justice of the particular case.

This becomes all the clearer in a juridical order which has a *codification of its centre*, for codifications, while they are nodal events in the history of a juridical order, are neither its beginning nor its end. In other words, a legal codex is not an extra-historical phenomenon.

Typically, law develops along the following lines[1]:

After a phase of systematising and collating (as in the case of a codification), the judicature and jurisprudence limit themselves for some time to exegesis. They are also motivated to do this by the authority (the legislature) behind the process of ordering and collating, which is generally convinced that its opus is timeless and has no lacunae. The more time goes on, the less the system is appropriate to solve new problems. Those who interpret the law, supported by jurisprudence, are more and more involved in actually creating law, until ultimately there is a call for a new systematic corpus for the sake of the stability of law. The latter demand will be all the more forceful if something crucial is changing in the foundations underlying the law.

The history of canon law since the 1917 CIC aptly corresponds to this typical sequence of events, particularly bearing in mind the significance of Vatican II. However, the new Codex exhibits a series of special features which present the possibility of the development of law being permanently open; this would also break the cycle of recurrence which is so typical of 'codex law'.

What are these features? John Paul II begins his promulgatory constitution with the words: 'As time goes on, the Catholic Church is accustomed to change and renew the laws of ecclesial living, so that, while maintaining faithfulness to the divine Founder, they may minister appropriately to the mission of slavation with which it is entrusted'. In the Preface to the Codex this idea is put even more clearly: 'If, as a result of today's rapidly changing human society, some things in this canon law are already less perfect than they might be, and will eventually call for revision, the Church is so richly endowed with abilities that, as in past centuries, it will be able once more to embark upon a renewal of the laws of its life'.

This view of the necessity of changing and renewing law as time goes by— which is not typical of codifiers in general—must in my view be seen in the context of the reference to Vatican II. Here we should turn once more to the promulgatory constitution, where we read: '... after all these considerations one may well hope that the new canon law will be an effective instrument which the Church can use to perfect itself according to the spirit of the Second Vatican Council, and can increasingly show itself fit to fulfil its saving mission in this world'. Such a task can only be carried out by a free and open development of law, not by a positivist interpretation of the letter in the manner of traditional exegesis.

Here there arises a difficulty, however, which results from the incoherent picture of the Church found in the 1983 CIC. All commentaries on the new Codex—except those that content themselves with establishing its legal-doctrinal content—are agreed that it is shaped by a *juxtaposition of two ecclesiologies*, on the one hand that based on the traditional 'societas perfecta' view, and on the other the 'communio' ecclesiology revived by Vatican II.

Basically there are two different reasons given for this. For some, the Codex here reveals its transitional character. They see the Codex as being compiled at a time when the implications of the 'communio' ecclesiology for canon law have not yet been fully grasped. Future development, therefore, would be in the direction of extending the 'communion' ecclesiology to all areas of canon law. The task referred to in the promulgatory decree (i.e., that the Church may be rendered more perfect, with the help of canon law, in the spirit of Vatican II) could doubtless be understood in this way.

The other approach in understanding the coexistence of the two ecclesiologies can be put like this: *Lumen gentium* (§ 8) speaks of the Church as a complex reality which also comprises a society in this world, with an appropriate order and constitution. Hence there is an *interplay of 'societas' and 'communio'* such as is expressed in canon 204: the Church as 'communio', as soon as it acquires a tangible order and constitution in the world, automatically takes on the character of a 'societas'.

In my view, canon 204 reverses the old tag, '*ubi societas, ibi jus*' and renders it, '*ubi jus, ibi societas*'. In other words, it is not because the Church is a society that a juridical order must follow: it is because the 'communio' of the Church, once it is visibly and tangibly in the world, calls for a juridical order, that it is constituted and ordered as a 'societas'. Behind this stands the conviction that juridical order is only possible within the framework of the traditional 'societas'.

However, the retention of elements of the 'societas' ecclesiology is inseparable from a *particular* concept of law. This concept was formed in modern secular jurisprudence, culminating in the various positivist approaches of the last hundred years, a development which exhibits a feedback relationship with the emergence of the modern concept of the State. As is well known, the doctrine of the 'societas perfecta' arose out of the Catholic Church's *twofold confrontation*, with the *Reformation*, and with the *modern State*. The Church had to assert its autonomy and equal status in the face of the omnicompetent modern State. But the result of this, particularly in the nineteenth and far into the twentieth centuries, was that it adopted substantial elements of the concept of law associated with this idea of the State. This development reached a climax in the concept of law of twentieth century Italian canonists, which was closely dependent on positivist jurisprudence.

Here law is understood as a closed system, established according to formal, abstract criteria, in order to serve an exaggerated emphasis on its stability. A functionalist approach such as this finds it easy to operate with a hierarchical

Church system where there are superiors and subordinates. It is no surprise that this concept, in the secular sphere, originated in the period of enlightened absolutism.

We should not overlook the fact, however, that State democracy arose within the framework of this idea of law. It was linked with the hope that the combination of the democratic formation of opinion and wishes, and a formal concept of law—positivist jurisprudence—would bring about a freer and more just society which did not restrict the expression of views. Today we know that this hope was illusory, for such a society was unable to prevent the outbreak of totalitarian inhumanity.

The Church could not take the path of a fundamental democratisation, fraught with danger, within the framework of the 'societas perfecta' doctrine; it is not a possible path today and never will be. Nor is it a case of changing the Church into a formally democratic 'societas perfecta'. What has to be done is to facilitate the breakthrough of 'communio' ecclesiology in canon law.

In contrasting these two ecclesiologies, however, there is a danger to be avoided. Sobański sees 'societas' as an example of an exogenous model, whereas he regards 'communio' ecclesiology as endogenous to the Church.[2] Like many contemporary theologians in the field of law, he overlooks the fact that the *concept of 'communio' also has a history*, and one in which interdependence vis-à-vis the sphere of the State and the secular plays an important part.

This began with the *adoption of the Aristotelian teaching on 'koinonia' by the early Church*, and subsequently by High Scholasticism (through the Latin translations of Aristotle) and Humanism. The view of the Church as a 'communio sanctorum' had a great significance later on in the ·Reformation tradition; as a reaction to the rise of the modern State it led, in a secularised form, to the *separation of society and community*. F. Tönnies introduced this dichotomy by attributing permanent and genuine sharing of life, intimacy and a sense of worth, to 'community' (*Gemeinschaft*), whereas 'society' (*Gesellschaft*) was marked by a superficial and artificial symbiosis on the public plane. M. Scheler radicalised this approach in his social ideal of the 'community of love'.

One of the few canonists who were aware of these connections was W. Bertrams.[3] He is no doubt the originator of the explanation in the *nota praevia* to no. 2 of Lumen Gentium, which says that 'communio' should be understood not as 'a vague feeling, but as an organic reality which demands a juridical form and is at the same time animated by love'.

These extreme positions may well be obsolete in sociology, but all the same they can be detected in the various discussions of recent decades, particularly in the German-speaking area, on the principles underlying the social sciences; for instance, in the *debate between system-theory and critical theory*.

Let us consider the contemporary critique of purely formal democratic legitimation, of total state control; the desire for smaller, more graspable units, and for a genuinely democratic procedure which would safeguard the interests of all concerned. It cannot be denied that there is a connection between the success of 'communio' ecclesiology and these social developments. So exogenous factors do enter into the development of 'communio' ecclesiology, even if this fact is often obscured in the euphoria of recognition. It is naturally always easier to identify exogenous factors in the Church of the past than in the Church of the present; we are often inhibited in our evaluation of the latter. However, these observations should not lessen the importance of the task of putting 'communio' ecclesiology into effect.

With this in mind we must apply our critique to the twofold image of the Church found in the new Codex. It is clear from what we have said *why the two ecclesiologies are found in different books* of the Codex. Whereas Books II (in part), III and IV, which are the most important ecclesiologically, have a clear theological basis which presupposes faith as an epistemological principle and is founded on the understanding of the Church as 'communio', it is primarily the old 'societas' ecclesiology that lies behind Books I, V, VI and VII.[4]

Books III and IV (*munus sanctificandi* and *munus docendi*) contain those areas of juridical Church order which are fundamentally different from that of the State. Evidently, the theological context central to these books made it easier to part company with the 'societas' doctrine developed according to the model of State law.

This is also supported, however, by *Lumen gentium*, which devotes special sections to the People of God as sharing Christ's priestly office (LG § 10) and the prophetic office (LG § 12), whereas one looks in vain for a comparable statement with regard to the pastoral office.

Accordingly, the People of God appears as an active subject in Books II, III, and IV, though the idea is carried through consistently only in Books III and IV. Book II, with its central theme of the *munus regendi*, shows the new ecclesiology overlaying the old; in many places the old ecclesiology shows through.

The situation is quite different, however, where there are clear parallels to State law, significantly in Book I of the Codex. Here there are literal quotations from the 1917 Codex, most noticeably in the first title concerning law in the Church.

The report on the work of the *coetus studiorum de normis generalibus* clearly shows how these canons are still being understood as expressing *a juristic theory and method that are timelessly valid*.[5] This is how Castilio Lara, for example, justifies the adoption (unchanged) of many provisions of the *normae generales*, referring particularly to canon 17.[6] He describes the rules of interpretation contained therein as precise criteria, a view which was characteristic of positivist law theorists, but is hardly put forward by anyone in secular law theory nowadays. Above all, the criterion of the *propria verborum significatio* in the traditional sense seems no longer tenable. The normative meaning is not directly given in the legal text; it has to be arrived at, through argument, from the *interaction of text and life-situation*. 'There is no such thing as literal meaning as such, i.e., that could be established independently of the historical and changing reality to which it refers. To adopt a criterion such as the "literal meaning" would be willy-nilly to underwrite an arbitrary method of interpretation'.[7] The meaning of the words only arises, therefore, through argument, which involves the interaction of the text itself, seen through a layer of pre-judgments, with the concrete life-situation which is being evaluated.

A theory of the development of law based on 'communio' ecclesiology would need to provide a *hermeneutics of the process of interpretation* by showing the multiplicity of concrete factors which enter into this process. Argumentation according to the rules of practical discourse would have to be both offered and welcomed.

The task of canon law theory and methodology is to establish rules for such a process by determining the relationship between the concrete factors in the form of rules of argument. There is a strong canonist tradition for such a process in the mediaeval *regulae iuris*.[8]

At the present time the call for such a theory of interpretation makes itself heard primarily in American canon law, which, with regard to secular law, is not faced with a theory that is one-sidedly orientated to detailed provisions and codification.[9] Here too there is clearly a considerable degree of interdependence with relation to State law; there is nothing self-evident about the codification of law.

One of these rules of argument will have to read as follows: the burden of proof is in favour of arguments which express a link with the wishes of the legislator. Anyone pleading against this, e.g., on the grounds of individual justice for the good of souls, must bear the burden of proof and will have to show that practical discussion is possible on the plane of understanding of the Church community as it acts purposefully and in faith.[10]

It is also important here that all those affected should be involved in the Church's decision-making; this follows from the participation emphasised by *'communio'* ecclesiology. This is something that should be built in to the process as a safeguard. The right and the duty of all those affected to contribute to the discussion within the framework of the rules of the burden of proof, must be guaranteed.

What we find here in terms of almost unchanged formulations of the conditions for interpretation, is also manifest in the lack of reference to elements of *participation in the legal process*. The new Codex speaks neither of the fact that laws stand in need of being accepted, nor of the necessity of investigating particular aspects of legislation *ad experimentum*, nor of the right of appeal.

As far as the first is concerned, what we have is a mechanism that operates without any feedback. One can say, of course, that the attempt to establish precise conditions for for the acceptance of laws would entail huge, if not insuperable, difficulties; all the same it would be possible to envisage a multiplicity of ways in which the faithful could participate in the legislative process, both in the drawing up of law, prior to its promulgation, and afterwards too. According to the old canonist rule, *quod omnes tangit ab omnibus debet approbari*, it would have been possible to set down, in the Codex, the right of those affected to consultation prior to the promulgation of law.

An appeal procedure, following proper rules, could be envisaged to operate during the time before the law takes effect. If the needs of each regional church (and perhaps of even smaller units where particular legislation is concerned) are taken seriously, and that to which it testifies is accepted as a legitimate expression of its ecclesial reality, appropriate regulations would show that 'communio' ecclesiology had also penetrated the process of legislation. The right of appeal, correspondingly, would be the right of regional churches (or of smaller units in the case of particular laws) to raise objections to a norm, after having been invited, through its promulgation, to accept it.

At this point we can see the *protective function of procedures*, something which is often underrated in canon law. The right of appeal, of course, continues as a feature of doctrine in spite of the silence of the 1983 CIC, just as it survived the 1917 CIC. But its nature and scope were set forth in too diffuse and disunified a manner for it to attain any greater practical significance. The only way forward was to establish a regulated procedure, and those involved in the 1983 codification did not have the courage to attempt it.

Then there is the question of providing a special legal setting for legislation *ad experimentum*, which is not something that has come to an end with the appearance of the new Codex. Here too it will continue to be necessary to establish the particularities of this kind of legislation. One thinks, for instance, of mitigation in dispensation procedures, or of obligation on those affected to report on their experiences, which would thus contribute to a 'final' ruling.

Finally, in this connection we must also refer to *customary law*. It is well known that the 1983 CIC has brought about progress here in speaking of a 'custom introduced by a community of the faithful'. However, this does not mean that it has succeeded in relating *lex* and *consuetudo* in a way that corresponds to 'communio' ecclesiology. At the Congress of Canon Lawyers in Pamplona, W. Aymans expressed the view that 'the relationship of *lex* and *receptio*, and of *consuetudo* and *consensus*, must be seen as a jurisprudential dimension of the Church's theological nature and its specific life-form'.[11] Such a view did not succeed in establishing itself in the Codex.

The continuing reservations with regard to customary law are clearly evident in a correction—striking one as petty—made during the last stages of codification. Whereas the draft Codex reduced the term for the validation of customary law from 40 years (in the old Codex) to 20, the final version increased this again to 30 years. Given the dynamism of our society, which is so marked by the multiplicity of communications, a 30-year term is almost equivalent to a deliberate block. Nonetheless, canon law must continue to devote more attention to customary law.

A further example of the interrelatedness of 'societas' doctrine, a particular concept of the State and the corresponding jurisprudence can be seen in the much-debated question of *constitutional rights in the Church*.

Those who deny any parallel with constitutional rights in the State do so by saying that there the issue is one of rights to freedom: the human being is to be guaranteed an area of freedom prior to the claims of the State, on the basis of his inherent dignity.[12] It would seem plausible that such a view cannot be transplanted into the idea of constitutional rights in the Church, for here there can be no question of creating an exclusion zone around the religious subject in which the Church cannot interfere.

As Luf has recently shown,[13] the weakness of this argument is that it is based on the understanding of constitutional rights stemming from the second half of the nineteenth century. The history of constitutional rights shows, by contrast, that the primary purpose is to create those legal and institutional conditions under which the subject can develop as a free and responsible individual in the State, and to provide him with appropriate opportunities to participate in shaping a common will. The function of protection from arbitrary State interference is an important corollary of this. If constitutional rights are understood in this way, an analogous concept could indeed be applied in canon law. It would be seen as an 'institutional order, legally formulated, regulating the fundamental ecclesial relationships (kerygmatic, sacramental and apostolic) in such a way that the communio and its members can fulfil their basic ecclesial potentialities in freedom'.[14]

Thus constitutional rights will have to be seen as a factor promoting the life of the community of the Church;[15] only then will canon law in its entirety have a chance, in the future, of exercising a formative and regulative influence on the reality of the People of God in this world.

Translated by Graham Harrison

Notes

1. W. Fikentscher *Methoden des Rechts* (Tübingen 1975) I pp. 5 ff.
2. R. Sobański 'Modell des Kirche-Mysteriums als Grundlage der Theorie des Kirchenrechts' in *AfkKR* 125 (1976) p. 22 f.
3. W. Bertrams 'Communio, communitas et societas in lege fundamentali ecclesiae' in *Periodica de re morali canonica liturgica* LXI (1972) 576 ff.
4. H. Müller 'COMMUNIO ALSO KIRCHENRECHTLICHES Prinzip im Codex Iuris Canonici von 1983?' in *Im Gespräch mit dem dreieinigen Gott* (Düsseldorf 1985) pp. 483 ff.
5. *Communications* XV (Rome 1984) 143 ff.
6. R. Castillo Lara 'Criteria di lettura e comprensione del nuove Codice: Il nuovo Codice di diritto canonico' in *Utrumque ius IX* (Rome 1983) 23.
7. H. Pree *Die evolutive Interpretation der Rechtsnorm im Kanonischen Recht* (Vienna/New York 1980) p. 220.
8. V. Bartocetti *De Regulis juris canonici* (Rome 1955).
9. J.A. Coriden 'Rules for Interpreters' in *The Jurist* 42 (1982) 277.
10. R. Potz 'Die Geltung kirchenrechtlicher Normen' in *Kirche und Recht* 15 (Vienna 1978) 264 f: 'In this communio the *sensus fidelium* is operative, expressing the *sensus fidelium* is determined by the intention of those who act in faith. Through this faith-oriented intention the People of God is placed in a theonomous frame of reference. In being aware of this frame of reference we are aware of a truth which is given; it is not something the Church can manufacture. The community of the Church, acting in faith, also understands in faith the transcendental conditions for the possibility of the truth of a consensus of agents in communication with one another. Behind the plane on which action informed by faith leads to truth, there is no meta-plane where actions of the Church could be subject to human evaluation; such action can only be referred to the grace and justification of God'.
11. W. Aymans 'Die Quellen des kanonischen Rechtes in der Kodification von 1917' in *La Norma en el Derecho Canonico I* (Pamplona 1979) pp. 487 ff.
12. W. Aymans 'Kirchliche Grundrechte und Menschenrechte' in *AfkKR* 149 (1980) pp. 389 ff.
13. G. Luf 'Grundrechte im CIC 1983' in *ÖAKR* 35 (1985).
14. P. Hinder *Grundrechte in der Kirche* (Fribourg, Switzerland 1977).
15. R. Sobański 'Recht unnd Freiheit des in der Taufe wiedergeborenen Menschen' in *La Norma en el Derecho Canonico I* (Pamplona 1979) pp. 877 ff.

Peter Huizing

The Central Legal System and Autonomous Churches

THE IDEA of the Church as a perfect society—*societas perfecta*—predominated up until the Second Vatican Council in discussions of public canon law (i.e. that part of canon law dealing with the constitution of the Catholic Church and its relationship with States) and in the administration of the Church. This concept served as the basis for the Church having a legal order of its own. Its content can be expressed in the following legal terms: (1) alongside, above and independent of the legal systems of secular States, the Roman Catholic Church forms a universal, sovereign, autonomous religious legal order; (2) this is based on the pope's universal legal power over the entire Church, represented in the dioceses, the Church's administrative subdivisions, by bishops appointed by the pope for the execution of his goverment; (3) the 'lower clergy' and the faithful, the 'Roman Catholics', constitute passive subjects under this hierarchy of popes and bishops.

The Councii provided substantial corrections to these points, to the extent that they depart from the Christian tradition.

1: THE UNIVERSAL CHURCH—A COMMUNITY OF LOCAL CHURCHES

By 'local churches' is understood first of all the dioceses and the churches equated with them, whether on a territorial or group basis. According to the context 'local Church' can also mean every religious community that has a social organisation, such as parish, deanery, the area covered by a bishops' conference, an ecclesiastical province, and the churches of larger cultural areas with some form of co-operation, such as Latin America, Africa, India.

Although in its constitution on the Church (*Lumen gentium*) the Council was dealing directly with the college of bishops it also in that context makes a fundamental statement about the relationship between the universal Church and the local churches: 'The individual bishops are the visible source and foundation of unity in their own particular churches, which are constituted after the model of the universal Church; it is in these and formed out of them that the one and unique Catholic Church exists' (*Lumen gentium* § 23).

The one Church exists in *the local churches*

What it means for a Church to exist is expounded by the Council at the start of its constitution on the liturgy. God's work of salvation, accomplished by Christ and his deeds, is maintained in the Church and realised in its liturgy by the presence of Christ himself (*Sacrosanctum Concilium* § 5–7). This Church becomes most clearly visible in the participation of the people in the same liturgical celebrations, the same eucharist, the one prayer, the one altar, whether together with the bishop (§ 41), whether usually in parishes, which 'in some way represent the visible Church constituted throughout the world' (§ 42). In coming together to celebrate the eucharist the faithful give concrete shape to the unity of the people of God, a unity which is at one and the same time given visible expression and brought about by the Eucharist (*Lumen gentium* § 11).

In the local churches this life that has been created and nourished by God is lived visibly and concretely, and in its entirety, although, to use Paul's terminology, Christ is not divided among the churches. From this point of view there is no difference at all between the local churches: they are all of completely the same standing, and there is no distinction of higher or lower among them.

This provides substantial correction to the view of the local Church as an administrative division of the universal Church within which the bishop has power of government. The decree on the pastoral office of bishops in the Church defines a diocese as a part of the people of God under the leadership of a bishop and his priests so that, united in the Holy Spirit by the gospel and the Eucharist together with the bishop and through his pastoral oversight, it forms a local church in which the one, holy, catholic and apostolic Church of Christ is truly present and active (*Christus Dominus* § 11; see canon 369).[1]

The one Church exists out of *the local churches*

The universal Church is a community of churches. This community rests on the same foundation as the community inside the local churches: the Spirit of Father and Son sent by the Father to the Church of his Son, who is also for this community 'the principle of their union and unity in the teaching of the apostles and fellowship, in the breaking of bread' (*Lumen gentium* § 13). The most essential foundation of the community of all the churches is thus its own essential nature. The universal representation of this is the community of the bishops together with the bishop of the church of Rome. In this sense the popes can be called the visible principle and foundation of the unity of the bishops and the multitude of the faithful, and the bishops the visible principle and foundation of the unity of their local Churches (*Lumen gentium* § 13). Paul admittedly preferred to call them not the foundation but God's fellow-workers or master-builders, workers and builders on the one foundation: 'For no other foundation can any one lay than that which is laid, which is Jesus Christ'. Both the local churches and the universal Church as their community are and remain primarily 'God's field, God's building' (1 Cor. 3:9–11). The visibility of the one Church in its hierarchical structure is based on the fundamental visibility of its one confession of faith around its one Eucharist.

2: THE BISHOPS OF ROME AND THE OTHER BISHOPS[2]

The office of bishop

In the model of the Church as a 'perfect society' this picture is predominantly based on the papal 'fullness of power'—*plenitudo potestatis.* In the episcopal ministry a distinction is made between the power of ordination and the power of government. The bishop receives the first in his own sacramental ordination, whereby he obtains 'power' to perform the 'sacred' actions of ordaining priests and bishops and administering confirmation. His power of government he receives through the *missio canonica* on his appointment by the Pope.

This idea was the result of centuries of development that diverged more and more strongly from an original tradition that itself lasted for centuries. In the first centuries bishops were elected by their own ecclesial communities, clergy and people together, and afterwards ordained by bishops of neighbouring Churches: in the name of the Lord and in his Spirit they were appointed to their one indivisible office as presidents at the liturgy, proclaimers of the gospel and administrators of their own ecclesial community. It was only from the later middle ages onwards that gradually in the Latin Church the appointment of bishops was reserved more and more to the popes and finally became their exclusive right; with the result that the separation between administrative appointment and *missio canonica*, on the one hand, and, on the other, sacramental ordination led to the idea of the two 'powers' in the episcopal ministry.

Here too the Council has restored the authentic tradition, at least in principle. Just as the apostles received from Jesus his Spirit for their one apostolic mission, and they imparted this Spirit to their fellow-workers by the laying on of hands, so too episcopal ordination transmits the fullness of the laying on of hands, so too episcopal ordination transmits the fullness of the episcopal ministry as a united office of sanctifying, teaching and governing: an office that naturally is transmitted and accepted in fellowship with the other churches and their bishops (*Lumen gentium* § 21; canon 375 § 2). Through the Holy Spirit that is bestowed on them the bishops are teachers, priests and shepherds (*Christus Dominus* § 2). Even the bishop of Rome discharges his office, after acceptance of his election, by virtue of his ordination: should someone who is not a bishop be elected pope, then he must receive his mission as quickly as possible through episcopal ordination (canon 332 § 1).

Hence the normal and daily care for their churches is committed to the bishops not as deputies for the bishops of Rome but as possessing an authority of their own that is not suppressed by the pope's universal authority but on the contrary confirmed, strengthened and defended by it (*Lumen gentium* § 21). By virtue of their office they are competent to act on their own responsibility, a competence which they need, without prejudice to the competence of the pope to reserve certain matters to himself or to other authorities: this as a rule can only apply to matters that really affect the general interest and leave the bishop's normal competence intact. Within this is also understood the competence to dispense their faithful from general laws of the Church as long as they regard this as necessary for their spiritual well-being, obviously with the reservation already mentioned: a competence previously only conceded in emergencies (*Christus Dominus* § 8; canon 87 §§ 1–2).

The college of bishops

Under the heading 'The supreme power and those who share in it by the law of the Church', the 1917 code of canon law dealt in separate chapters first with the pope and then with the general council, leaving undecided whether this latter derived its authority from divine or ecclesiastical law. Following the Council (*Lumen gentium* §§ƒ 23, 25) the 1983 code puts the two together under the heading: 'The Roman pontiff and the college of bishops'. The canons on the authority of the pope are followed by those on the college of bishops, together with the pope, of course, and to this college too is ascribed the highest authority in the universal Church. Moreover, while the Council emphasises the essential link of the other bishops with the pope (*Lumen gentium*, ibid.), the code of canon law explicitly establishes that in the exercise of their ministry they are alwasy linked with the other bishops and indeed with the entire Church (canon 333 § 2). Both the popes and the other bishops always act in and from the community of their apostolic college.

The bishops of the church of Rome, where Peter and Paul bore witness to Jesus with their lives and which from early days was the centre of the unity of all the Churches, have authority over all the churches and their bishops because of their special responsibility for this unity; and this as fellow-bishops, to which office they too in the early centuries were called by being elected by their own ecclesial community, clergy and people together (of which the election by the college of 'cardinals of the holy Roman Church' is still presented as the historical continuation), and installed in office in the name of the Lord through ordination by bishops of the neighbouring churches. The idea of a pope who is 'exempt', who does not have to be bishop of a local church and who would be elected and also ordained as universal bishop by a representative body of the universal Church, is so far removed from the Catholic tradition that it could never be accepted as a possible legitimate development. *There is no sacrament of ordination as a universal bishop.*

3: THE LOWER CLERGY AND THE LAITY

The Roman unitary model of 'the priest' also fitted into the idea of the Church as a perfect society. General law and central instructions governed his 'vocation', studies and training, his celibate way of life, his appointment, how he exercised his office, what he wore and the duties of his state. His job was concentrated on the administration of the sacraments and preaching, for which he was exclusively responsible to his bishop. He had to keep himself aloof from secular affairs. His own parishioners did not have any voice either in his ordination or in the exercise of his ministry. He was allotted to them as their mediator with God. His standing depended on his sacred power validly to consecrate and to forgive sins. The religious life of the laity was confined to attending and receiving the priest's ministry, practising the recommended individual virtues, making contributions to the Church's institutions (pretty well exclusively run by priests and above all by members of religious orders) for education, the care of the sick and the poor, missionary work and similar, and ultimately participation in the life of Catholic organisations, where the 'spiritual advisor' provided the one element that formally betokened the Church. The 'ecclesiastical' world of Church government and Church politics and the 'secular' world of the laity were separated and remained alien to each other. This very schematic sketch of some characteristic features of the system does not of course include any judgement on the personal religious life of priests and laity.

A complex of different converging factors led to a crisis in the system: the ending of the isolation of Catholic groupings in society and in the world; the transfer to secular society of many formerly Church institutions; awareness of the gulf between the ecclesiastical and secular worlds, which put many priests and lay-people in a kind of vacuum thanks to the former's onesidedly ecclesiastical education and the latter's religious education having remained underdeveloped in relation to their secular development; in brief the complex of factors that led to the process that is summed up in the term 'secularisation'.

Here too the Council, if at times with hesitation, has supported the development that has begun towards new relationships.

Priests

Some statements still recall the idea of the 'perfect society' in which the priests, on the analogy of the relationship between bishops and popes, were seen as representatives of the bishops: in the exercise of their ministry they depend on the bishop (*Lumen gentium* § 28); they are his aid and organ; they make him present among the faithful; they carry out his tasks and concerns; they must recognise and obey him as their father (*ibid.*); they are installed in office by the mission they have received from him and by ordination (*Presbyterorum ordinis* § 1); and it is in his name that they bring the family of God together (*Presbyterorum ordinis* § 6). Other statements tend instead to confirm the priest's independent position: with the bishops they share the dignity of the priesthood; by ordination they are set apart for preaching the gospel, shepherding the faithful, and worship (*Lumen gentium* § 28); they carry out their ministry in the name of Christ (*Presbyterorum ordinis* § 2); their office is bestowed on them through the sacrament whereby they are able to act 'in the person of Christ' (*ibid.*); through their ordination they receive the gift of the Holy Spirit; and they are the bishop's essential helpers and advisers. With all the emphasis on their duties towards the bishop the latter is instructed to listen to his priests, to ask their advice, to consult with them; and finally the priests are called the bishops' friends and brothers (*Presbyterorum ordinis* § 7).

The priest's independent role—and that of deacons and lay people in pastoral ministry—is determined by their direct link with the local communities in which they work. The bishop's role is clearly different from this. The idea that the pastoral care of parishes and groups of people is entrusted to pastoral workers alone because the bishop himself cannot be everywhere at once and do everything himself, though this should be the ideal, is absurd not only as a matter of obvious practical experience but also as a matter of principle: the diocesan church too only exists 'in' and 'out of' local churches with their own life, and the existence of these demands that they independently have at their disposal the pastoral ministries they need under the co-ordination of the bishop.

The laity

The place of the laity, the vast majority of the Church, was given more thorough consideration by the Council. The vision of the Church developed by *Lumen gentium* as the sign of the destiny of the people of God to which all men and women are called (chapter 2), and in whose service the hierarchy are given their mission (chapter 3), demands of itself an exposition of the role of the laity (chapter 4). The hierarchy has neither the mandate nor the ability to take on itself the Church's entire mission, but has the task of providing the ministry of leadership and inspiration for the individual mission of every one of the faithful with his or her own abilities (*Lumen gentium* § 30): in other words of lay men and women in the ordinary circumstances of family and society, and less simply as a 'secular order' opposed to the 'ecclesiastical order', which is equally a 'secular order'. The job of the laity too forms part of the work of 'one and the same Spirit' (1 Cor. 12:11) (*Lumen gentium* § 32). Their apostolate is an independent participation in the mission of the Church for which their mission comes from the Lord himself through baptism and confirmation (*Lumen gentium* § 33). They have the right and often the duty to give their judgment on the Church's internal affairs (*Lumen gentium* § 37). The pastoral constitution on the Church in the world of today—a comprehensive picture of the responsibility of the ecclesial community in the 'secular' society of marriage and family, culture, the economy, the social order, politics, international relations and the peace movement—throws new light on the authentic Christian meaning of the laity's work in the world. The decree on the lay apostolate develops the principles: among other things it underlines the autonomy of the laity in the secular order and their freedom of association even for directly apostolic enterprises (*Apostolicam actuositatem* § 19) and defines their relationship with the hierarchy (*Apostolicam actuositatem* § 24). The decree on the Church's missionary activity places special emphasis on the necessity of the lay apostolate for the local churches: the Church is not really established as the sign of Christ's presence among men and women, the gospel cannot really put down roots into a people's character, life and work, without the formation of a developed Christian laity (*Ad gentes* § 21).

Structures

As a structural support for co-operation in local churches the decree on the priestly life and ministry prescribes the setting up of a *council of priests* in every diocese as a·consultative organ representing all the priests working in the diocese (*Presbyterorum ordinis* § 7, canons 495–501). The decrees on the pastoral office of bishops·in the Church (*Christus Dominus* § 27) and on the lay apostolate (*Apostolicam actuositatem* §§ 24–26) express the Council's wish for pastoral councils of priests, religious and above all laity to be set up in dioceses and at other levels in the local churches (canons 511–514) and for a secretariat for the lay apostolate to be set up in Rome.

CONCLUSION

The question about the relationship of the Church's central legal system and the autonomy of the local Churches can be answered as follows on the basis of the Council statements that have been summarised above.

The *central* legislative function of general councils and popes and the *local* legislative function of governing colleges of bishops and diocesan bishops rest on the mission and responsibility bestowed on them at their ordination, something which they cannot assign or leave to other bodies. These functions should be fulfilled in the mutual community of the bishops of Rome with the other bishops, of the bishops among themselves, and of the diocesan bishops with the clergy and people of their churches, and legislation should be the result of a collegial process of making up one's mind and taking decisions, a process in which the independent contribution of the churches and groups affected genuinely plays its full part. The aim of all Church legislation is simply to protect and encourage the independent life of faith and fellowship in the actual local churches—what the old Latin phrase described as *salus animarum*, the salvation of souls.

The Catholic Church's legal structure can be neither monarchic nor democratic. Thanks to its nature as a community or fellowship of local churches its legal structure can only be that of a community in which the mission and equal dignity of everyone is respected and protected by everyone. Every distortion of this balance necessarily upsets the mission of the Church itself. The Church does indeed remain a fellowship of earthly men and women and disturbances will thus always occur, but it remains necessary to anticipate these as much as possible and to repair the damage. It is finally the legal structure of a fellowship which would abandon its mission if it did not continue to strive for the fulfilment of the prayer 'that they may all be one' (John 17:11).

Translated by Robert Nowell

Notes

1. Hervé Legrand 'La réalisation de l'Église en un lieu' in *Initiation à la pratique de la théologie*, publié sous la direction de Bernard Lauret et Froncçois Refoulé, III, *Dogmatique* 2 (Paris 1983) 145–329, with bibliography at pp. 330–345: a study embracing all aspects of this subject.
2. J.M. Tillard *The Bishop of Rome* (London 1983) (a well documented theological study); Patrick Granfield *The Papacy in Transition* (New York 1980); various authors *Das Papstamt. Dienst oder Hindernis für die (Ökumene?, (Regensburg 1985).*

Francis Morrisey

Is the New Code an Improvement for the Law of the Catholic Church?

THE NEW Code of Canon Law was the result of one of the most extensive and painstaking consultative enterprises carried out by the Catholic Church. But in spite of the extensive consultations, as with any text of law, it will be nearly impossible to satisfy everyone. What counts most is that the majority feel that the new code is adequate for their ordinary needs and expectations.

The code reflects a given moment in the life and history of the Church, as well as a certain vision of Church. It has no pretence of being the final word on the matters it contains. The law builds on the life and tradition of the Church; law must follow life, not create it.

At the outset is must be noted that the new code has met with surprising interest in many parts of the world. There have been numberous sessions for lay persons, bishops, priests and religious. Many weeks have been devoted to its study and gradual implementation. In other words, the new code is undoubtedly responding to a wide-felt need. Of course, it will take ten years or more before local legislation to implement the law properly has been enacted and applied; but already the long process has begun.

An evaluation of the new code at this moment in its history can focus on three general areas: the thrust of the law itself; positive aspects of the new legislation; points which will require adaptation or substantial change in the years ahead.

I. THE THRUST OF THE NEW LAW

Any text of law must meet a number of generally accepted pre-determined criteria. So it is with the new Code.

(a) One of the purposes of legislation is to promote the *common good* and to help avoid the arbitrary, which is one of the worst forms of dictatorship. Good law should spell out the purposes of a society, the structures to be used to attain these goals, and the rights and obligations of the group's members. It is evident that the new code meets these criteria.

(b) The *principles* to be observed in preparing the new code were overwhelmingly approved by the first Synod of Bishops in 1967. The law should be evaluated within the context of these criteria, not in light of some utopian vision that cannot become a reality given the human situation of the Church. One of the ten principles was not fully translated into reality in the text, that of providing adequate means of redress when rights of Church members were not respected; the proposals to establish administrative tribunals in each diocese were not incorporated into the final version of the law. This principle aside, the nine other principles were fairly well implemented.

(c) The Code is to be a *text of law*, not a compendium of theology or manual of spirituality. But it necessarily depends on the current state of theology for many of its orientations. If some theological questions remain unanswered, it would be unreasonable to expect a law text to resolve the discussion. Three particular areas remain open ended because much study remains to be done to fine tune a number of doctrinal principles.

The first concerns the *sacraments and ministry*. Each sacrament, without exception, still gives rise to significant doctrinal and theological questions. The Code had to reflect this developing state. Moreover, the Code wisely avoids legislation about new ministries for the reason that they are new.

A second area concerns the *relationships between pope and bishops*, with the intermediate reality of the episcopal conferences. Some first steps have been taken toward redefining the position and role of the diocesan bishop in the particular church entrusted to his care (See *LG* 27). But there are still many unanswered questions, particularly as regards mandatory reference to the supreme authority of the Church in certain issues and the extent to which decisions of the episcopal conference bind a bishop who does not agree with them.

A third area concerns the *relationships of the Church with other Christian churches*. While a number of interesting steps were incorporated in the new law, particularly in regard to canon II, it would have been unrealistic to expect further developments until we have reached greater agreement on many doctrinal points.

(d) Furthermore, the Code cannot be expected to resolve *problems arising from personalities and human situations*. No amount of legislation can give good judgment to a person, or can make someone kind, compassionate, or understanding. Even though a canon might be formulated in an ideal fashion, its application will depend on many human factors.

Therefore, an overall evaluation of the new Code is positive. There are also specific positive elements which can be singled out.

2. POSITIVE ELEMENTS

A number of interesting minor changes have been incorporated into the new law, but these are often only details. There is, however, *a much deeper renewal in the spirit* underlying the legislation. It is this spirit which helps provide for the newness of the Code It could be summed up as follows: the law, whose purpose is to deepen the work of the Spirit within the Church, derives its inspiration from the doctrine of the Church. This doctrine, for the most part, was formulated and taught by the Second Vatican Council. For this reason Pope John Paul II has stated on many occasions that the code is 'the last of the Vatican II documents' (allowing, of course, for its companion document for the Eastern Churches). The application of this renewed doctrinal spirit can be seen in many sections of the law.

(a) A Renewed Ecclesiology

Canons 204-207, along with canon 369, express in few words a renewed vision of Church, one centred on the people of God comprised of all the baptised—the faithful. The Code distinguishes between the Church of Christ and its practical expression in the Catholic Church (see canons 204, §2 and 369). Recent popes have spoken of our 'sister churches' which also share in many regards in ecclesial realities.

Special emphasis is placed on the diocese or particular church. In it the one, holy, catholic and apostolic Church of Christ truly exists and functions (can. 369). The communion of the various churches makes up the '*Ecclesia universa*' (can. 749) or the entire Church. This renewed emphasis places special obligations on the diocese to incarnate the reality of Church, and on religious whose apostolate must be coordinated with that of the diocese where they exercise their mission.

The Code does not always seem to be consistent in its use of the word 'faithful' (see canons 204, 492, 918, etc.); it still focuses on baptism as the means of incorporation into the Church (can. 96). What is different is the emphasis placed on the call to mission which flows from baptism and not from the sacrament of orders. All the faithful (clergy, religious, laity) are called to mission (to teach, sanctify and serve) because of their incorporation into Christ through baptism. It would be wrong to state that the new code speaks of the 'Church of the laity'; rather, it speaks of the Church of the 'faithful', of which the laity are necessarily part.

The ecclesiology focuses more particularly on the model of the Church as a 'communion'. While the code relies on such notions as hierarchical communion, the communion of believers and the communion of the churches, it also (and more particularly) speaks of those who are in full communion with the Catholic Church here on earth (can. 205), of those who are in partial communion (c. 844), those who are not in communion (can. 1331), or who are no longer in communion (cf. can. 117).

(b) Word and Sacrament

One striking characteristic of the new code is the renewed emphasis placed on the Word of God. It is especially through the ministry of the Word that fiath is brought into existence and strengthened (can. 836). The faithful have the right to be assisted by their pastors with the Word of God and the sacraments (can. 213). The diocese is centered on the gospel and the Eucharist (can. 369); the parish priest's duties regarding the Word are spelled out in canon 538, §1, while those regarding the sacraments are found in §2 of the same canon.

Book III of the code is devoted entirely to the ministry of the Word on its various forms, while Book IV centres on the sacraments. Both of these are seen as applications of the Church's missions of teaching and sanctifying.

The justice ministry in the Church is seen as an outreach of the ministry of the Word (can. 528, §1). This particular form of ministry must flow from true gospel principles and not simply from an emphasis on various causes to be promoted.

(c) Charter of Rights

One creative aspect of the new code is the emphasis placed on fundamental rights in the Church. The charter of rights is presented in four sections, along with corresponding obligations: the obligations and rights of all the faithful (canons 208–223), of the laity (canons 224–231), of the clergy (canons 273–289), and of religious (canons 662–672). After the promulgation of the code a section on the rights of the family was issued.

As with any bill of rights, it will take time to see what practical significance they will have in the life of the Church. They will probably be the means whereby the new code will ultimately bring about a change in mentality in many areas of Church life.

(d) Concern for Culture

It is difficult to take into account the various cultural factors that the Church faces in proclaiming the message of salvation throughout the world. The fact that something is part of a culture does not necessarily make it right or wrong. Each of these factors has to be weighed and examined individually.

Native character and culture must be taken into account so as to open up new ways which can lead to the gospel (can. 787). This is also evident in the cultural upbringing of children (can. 1136) and in the various canons which refer to local customs (cf. canons 396, §2; 423, §1; 1076; etc.).

By providing possibilities of local adaptations either by the episcopal conference, the diocesan bishop, or the particular institute of consecrated life, the Code allows for many adjustments in sacramental and liturgical matters, in diocesan organisation, and in the formation of candidates to priesthood and lay ministries.

As time goes on it will become increasingly more difficult for the Church to have a universal law. The 1983 Code might well be one of the last such instruments the Church will have if it wishes to remain truly catholic. The awakening of true self-identity in the newer churches will necessarily call for some type of adaptation of Church law to particular situations. However, even in those churches where Catholics are fewer in numbers, it is not a simple matter to agree on which points are generally accepted by all as being truly expressive of a given culture. Thus, for instance, to speak of an 'African' or a 'Southern African' notion of marriage would be to ignore the complex realities of the region.

The concern for culture is particularly evident in the canons on marriage which use general terms to describe fundamental attitudes. Such expressions as 'the good of the spouses', 'the partnership of the whole of life', and 'the irrevocable covenant' can find practical applications in varying cultures.

(e) An Emphasis on Mission

Many canons refer to the mission of Christ as entrusted to the Church. The threefold mission of teaching, sanctifying and serving provides a basic framework for the various books of the Code.

Because of baptism, and consequent membership in the people of God, a person is called to share in the mission which was entrusted to the Church to fulfill in the world (can. 204). In a very significant change of perspective, the call to mission arises from the sacraments of baptism and confirmation (can. 225); under the previous legislation, authority in the Church came from the sacrament of orders, thus giving a clerical vision to the Church.

A similar shift of emphasis is found in the norms on the exercise of authority—the royal mission—which is now presented as a service (can. 618). Instead of a domineering attitude over persons who are considered as subjects, the Code calls for an attitude of respect for others, based on their dignity (can. 618).

(f) Consecrated Life

One of the biggest challenges facing the Commission was to prepare a law for consecrated life that would protect and enhance the charism of each institute. While individual canons do not always meet every expectation, nevertheless a challenge is offered to each institute to identify its patrimony (can. 578) and charism, and then faithfully to protect it.

Many institutes will be unable to agree on what constitutes their fundamental charism; but this is not the fault of the law. Those institutes that cannot do so have little chance of survival.

The fact that many canons refer to the particular law of the institute avoids a levelling among communities that the 1917 Code unwittingly fostered. What will be of prime importance, however, is for each institute to identify clearly its nature, and to adjust its life style accordingly. It could be asked, though, whether the Code's criteria identifying each type of institute (religious and secular) are appropriate and not too rigid.

Nevertheless, the new legislation for institutes of consecrated life is generally far superior to what was previously in effect. It offers a fascinating challenge to each institute to determine what it has to offer the particular church.

(g) Financial Administration

The financial law of the Church, particularly Book V, has been substantially revised to take into account not only the various civil laws existing in a territory, but also new means of financial organisation.

Both the bishop and the parish priest are to be freed of the general duties of day to day administration so they can devote their efforts to Word and sacrament. For instance, the detailed description of the parish priest's duties (canons 528-529) make no reference to financial matters.

There is a particular concern in Book V for justice, respect of donors' intentions, and for observance of relevant civil legislation This concern is of particular import because the credibility of the Church's statements on such matters depends to a great extent on what it does itself.

3. MATTERS THAT WILL CALL FOR RECONSIDERATION

While there are many positive features in the new code which far outweigh the negative ones, nevertheless there remain a number of points which could be improved. We can briefly mention only a few.

(a) Compromises and Ambiguities

While it was nearly impossible for the law to resolve disputed points, particularly those which flow from a theology still in the process of formation, some canons which are necessarily compromises will raise more questions than they solve.

Primary among these is canon 129, §2: laity may cooperate in the *mission of governing* according to the norms of law. Although the code elsewhere speaks of the call to mission arising from baptism (canons 104, 155), it still retains a clerical image in many areas where this would not be necessary. Events may soon overtake the letter of the law, making it somewhat irrelevant.

Another example of a compromise is found in the *exclaustration of religious* (can. 687). In such an important matter the law is frustratingly vague. A remarkable inconsistency appears in all clerics being bound to perfect continence and celibacy (can. 277); no exception was made for married deacons who are also clerics.

(b) Relations with Other Rites and Churches

The code has made interesting advances in the question of relations with other churches. However, there are still a number of ambiguities. For instance, some surprising consequences come from recognising the Orthodox form of marriage: a marriage between an Oriental Catholic who is not subject to a Latin bishop and an Orthodox will not be valid if celebrated by a Catholic Latin rite bishop, although the same would be valid if celebrated before an Orthodox priest who is not in full communion with the Catholic Church (canons 1109, 1127).

(c) Lay Involvement in Councils and Synods

While the code foresees that lay people may be invited to councils and synods—and this is an excellent improvement—it still speaks of such lay persons in rather patronising terms. Reference is made to lay persons of 'outstanding integrity', 'probity of life', 'above suspicion', 'of good repute' (see canons 483, 1064, 1424, 1435). The same should also have been applied to clerics and religious. Also, is it still appropriate that the code does not come down strongly in favour of lay participation?

While continuing to proclaim that we are the people of God, with basic equality of dignity and action (can. 208), the mode of operation remains clerical in perspective. There are openings, but they are still cautious. Pastoral councils are optional (canons 511, 536); the possibility of lay membership on committees is open (cf. can. 492); lay involvement is sometimes only in case of necessity (cf. canons 517, 861, 1112, 1421).

(d) Women in Church Law

Remarkable progress was made in regard to the situation of women in Church law—leaving aside the question of orders, which is more a theological than a canonical one. But there are still canons which are difficult to justify.

For instance, it is difficult to provide a justification for retaining the prescription against women being eligible for the ministries of lector and acolyte (can. 230). On the other hand, the Code provides for the consecration of lay women to the service of the diocesan church (can. 604), but no similar rite exists for a man who would wish to consecrate his life in this way without joining the clergy or an institute of consecrated life.

The canon on abduction (can. 1089) could have been reworked to cover both men and women, particularly in cases of entrapment. The structures of lay institutes of consecrated life (both of men and of women) still raise some questions in reference to ordinaries; there is a dependence here that could be reexamined at some future date.

(e) Procedures

Undoubtedly for many the most unsatisfactory part of the new Code is Book VII on procedures. The canons have many examples of 'overkill' (see canons 1598, 1673, 1689, etc.). It can be asked whether the Church really wants marriage nullity cases to proceed, notwithstanding its proclamation of the right of all Catholics to have their state of life recognised (canons 1400, 1445, 1492, 1691). Many fear this approach will have the effect in some places of leading to extra-judicial 'solutions', something that could be far more arbitrary than any of the so-called 'abuses' the Commission wished to address.

(f) Administrative Tribunals

Although the Code speaks of the possibility of administrative tribunals, it does not make them mendatory (see can. 1733). Where such are not established, it can be asked what redress exists for Catholics who feel aggrieved in the exercise of their rights. It might not be surprising to see them taking grievances to civil courts for resolution.

(g) Religious

Despite positive features in the law for consecrated life, there are still unrealistic expectations regarding the living of community life. Many religious are simply unable to live in community because of the demands of the apostolate. The law could certainly have been more flexible in this regard, and with regard to absences from the novitiate.

The way the evangelical counsel of obedience is expressed raises a number of questions (can. 601). Is it possible to vow to bind oneself to submission of will to lawful superiors? It would have been preferable to speak of obeying the orders of such superiors without entering the realm of the internal forum.

(h) The Role of Episcopal Conferences

One potential benefit of the new Code could lie in the significance given to local decisions, particularly those of episcopal conferences. However, if a conference is unable or unwilling to act, many things will remain in abeyance. The requirement that decrees of the conference be reviewed by the Holy See could be seen to be unnecessary centralisation (can. 455).

CONCLUSION

This overview of trends in the new Code and of some potential weaknesses shows, I believe, that at this particular time in the life of the Church, the Code is an improvement over he previous legislation. But it does not resolve all outstanding issues.

We would have been justified in hoping for something better, but it might have been unrealistic to expect the Church to move too quickly. There will undoubtedly be pressure for changes in the legislation, at least on certain points. But it would probably take another council, or something similar, before any significant revision could take place.

What probably counts most now is for all involved in applying the Code to do so to the utmost of their possibilities, using every avenue the Code opens. If the experience then proves positive, it will be easier to press for a further change in some of the canons. In the meantime, we have available for those who wish to apply it a well thought-out pastoral instrument that enables us to assess where we are going and, especially, where we have come from. The supreme law is the salvation of souls (can. 1752); this will necessarily and ultimately prevail.

PART II

Particular Issues

Jean Bernhard

The New Matrimonial Law

ON 27 NOVEMBER 1986 the new Code of Canon Law will have been in force for three years. Already the editorial board of *Concilium* has asked us once again to examine matrimonial law: does that part of the 1983 Code answer the pastoral requirements of Christian communities? At the end of this first three years, its content does more than set bounds, for it also allows us to catch a glimpse of perspectives which deserve to be opened up.

Among the questions which face us straight away, one of the most important is certainly that of the *reception of the new Code.* The best interpretation of the Code is that offered by the actual life of the Church. The value of a code as of a tree is judged by the fruit which it bears. 'The Church lives from its base', according to Congar.

In a very real sense, the *Code is an unfinished phenomenon;* the importance of interpretation has to be stressed. To forbid interpretation would mean stopping still: an inability to confront the evolution of the world, the Church and society.

I do not intend to carry out an exegesis of codified texts, all the less because commentaries of this kind have already appeared. What I am offering is a re-reading of *De matrimonio,* in its continually updated capability to help order the life of the Church. In other terms, what is involved is helping to persuade local churches to make an enormous effort in regard to the active reception of the Code. In this sense, it is permissible to say that 'everything lies in execution and interpretation'.

Is it possible to discern *certain lines of force* in respect of what that reception might be in the area of marital law? We cannot give all the answers. The field is vast and we are still in the early stages. Tomorrow, as yesterday and today, we shall continue to 'fashion' the Code. A code which is conceived as 'movement' is a true drawing-power in the pilgrim Church.

In regard to my re-reading of matrimonial law, I must state at the outset that I am in France, at a moment of real transition to a new age of the Church and of society.

The way in which the human couple and marriage are conceived of is constantly developing before our very eyes. ' . . . Fewer and fewer marriages, more and more divorces, more and more unmarried unions, more and more single-parent families, more and more illegitimate children, more and more single people . . . . The about-face is unprecedented . . . in character, size and "speed"'.[1] Confronted with these new forms of marital behaviour, does the 1983 Code harden positions which as a whole remain faithful to the doctrine . of the 1917 Code, or does it prudently avoid questioning a 'post-Christian' society, leaving to canonical doctrine and pastoral theology the task of working out approaches to the situation and empirical solutions? Surely practice often comes before theory?

One of the basic criticisms of the new matrimonial law is often met with: Surely it is essentially a reaffirmation of the *one Western, Latin model* which all Catholics should take their bearings from? Whereas in reality, there is not one marriage but marriages. Any matrimonial model is essentially a cultural and historical phenomenon, relative to the society which helped to shape it.

In the 1983 Code, marriage is first *defined* as an 'intimate union for the whole of life', before the text lays down that, by its natural character, it is ordained for the procreation and upbringing of children: these two components are no longer presented as the 'chief end' of marriage; 'perpetual and exclusive rights over the body' of each partner with respect to the other gives way before the concept of the 'reciprocal gift and acceptance of two persons'. The *contractual terminology is maintained, alongside the term 'alliance'*, taken from the biblical and patristic tradition favoured by the second Vatican Council. As a whole, it is much more legal contract theory and not the sacramental reality, which continues to provide the basis of the canonical doctrine of marriage. As for impediments of marriage, they are almost exclusively deduced from 'natural law'.

Two questions are especially important in the present context: the *canonical form* of celebration of marriage, and the *content of the marriage commitment.*

1. THE CANONICAL FORM OF CELEBRATION OF MARRIAGE

Canons 1108-1115 of the new Code present the *canonical form* of the celebration of marriage as an entity which is extrinsic to marriage itself and purely legal in nature. In accordance with canon 1108 par. 2, however, anyone who 'assists at a marriage' acts in the name of the Church. It would appear that this text is a milestone on the way to a *more ecclesial conception of the couple's marriage commitment.* The recent development of the canonical doctrine of marriage (canons 1055 and 1057) represents major progress in regard to the 1917 Code. The new conception of marriage bears witness to a much greater degree of personalisation, a much deeper humanisation of love and marriage.

The main risk in this development would be its eventual location of the reciprocity of love solely in the private domain, thus ultimately devaluing such love and rendering it commonplace. The aim of this article is not to minimise the importance of interpersonal relations in contemporary marriages but to *re-value the communual and ecclesial dimension of Christian marriage.* Surely a personalist understanding of love and marriage implies the weight of institutional factors among the elements that go to make up marriage.

There are young couples who voluntarily state that they are not in the least interested in any official 'recognition', civil or religious, of their union. They say that institutions favour hypocrisy and destroy freedom. Yet often this rejection is accompanied by a need for acceptance of their new situation as cohabiting partners by the family and society. Certainly, then, from the anthropological viewpoint alone an interpersonal relationship cannot exist authentically unless it is integrated into a larger community. In short, the loving mutuality of a man and a woman becomes institutionalised not to lose its dynamism but to ensure that flourishes duly.

Christians live their conjugal partnership 'in the Lord'. The couple show forth the true meaning of love and are thus the duality of Christ and the Church. But the Christian people as a whole reflect God's own way of loving. The central thing is that it is not the couple who receive the sacrament of marriage, for *the couple become sacramental by being integrated into the 'sacramental' society of believers.* In the sacramental rite, the word of the couple is 'received' and welcomed by the community. That is to say: the entire community, and particularly married couples, should feel that they are participating in the spiritual undertaking of this young couple marrying 'in the Lord'.

The solidarity brought about between God and the couple is expressed in particular through the community. If this reciprocity does not exist, there is a lack. How many marriages have suffered setbacks because of an absence of support from the community.

Rather than adapt our sacramental pastoral approach to the 'privatisation' of marital love which characterises our contemporary society, I believe that the canonical form of celebration should rather make explicit the ecclesial dimension of the sacrament of marriage. The matrimonial commitment both establishes the couple and establishes the 'Church'.

The personal commitment of the spouses (towards one another, but also towards the community) is a commitment of the community towards the couple, and these ought to be the two constituent elements of a marriage's formation. The canonical form of celebration would then be a canonicolitur- gical form, the *personal and communitarian aspects of which would be intrinsically linked in a close relation.*

Therefore it is important that a marriage should be publicly acknowledged in the form of a mutual commitment of the two spouses before the ecclesial community (*in facie Ecclesiae*) and in the form of a commitment made by the community to the couple. A proposal of this kind would fully express the intention of canon 1063 of the new Code: 'Pastors of souls should ensure that their own ecclesial community offers the faithful a means of assistance in keeping the matrimonial state in the Christian spirit and in progressing in perfection'. No. 3 of the same canon states: 'The liturgical and fruitful celebration of marriage is intended to stress the fact that the partners are a sign of the mystery of unity and fruitfulness of love between Christ and the Church and that they share in that mystery'.

In any sacramental celebration, the minister (not necessarily the priest) intervenes in order to recall the fact that it is *God who actually effects the sacramental action.* There is apparently no reason why the sacrament of marriage should be excluded from the application of this principle, even if tradition is less tenacious in this area. Similarly, the word of God is vouch- safed to human beings to that they may have the word. The word of God asks the couple to live their marriage, in a special way, in the name of the Lord.

2. THE CONTENT OF MARITAL COMMITMENT

For the last twenty years, in France, *a growing concern for sincerity and authenticity* has inspired the pastoral interest in marriage. From being an almost exclusively legal procedure, it has passed into the state of an ecclesial practice, concerned more with the gospel and actual human beings than with the institution. Thereby the sacrament of marriage has run the risk, as an act of faith, of becoming a possibility reserved for Christians truly aware of their faith. For others, a number of theologians and pastors have opined, 'it is a matter of not burdening them with more than they can bear'. Why not advise them to enter into a purely civil marriage? Or rather, on certain conditions, a ceremony of welcome to the Church, it being made clear that this ceremony is not the sacrament of marriage. The drop in the number of marriages, and especially the decrease of the proportion of church marriages as compared with registry-office marriages would seem to reveal a trend to which the above mentioned pastoral approach is appropriate.

Effectively, the following questions arise nowadays: *Is marriage between baptised persons always raised to the level of a sacramental reality*? What are we to make of the marriage of two baptised persons who do not believe? Does baptism operate automatically? We know that the 1983 legislator refused to alter canon 1012 par. 2 of the 1917 Code: Between baptised persons, the new canon 1055 par. 2 repeats, the matrimonial contract cannot exist *validly* without being simultaneously a sacrament. The validity in question can only be a canonical validity. There is nothing in the way of canonical teaching recognising the canonical status of 'Catholics united by civil marriage alone'. There is no longer any mention of concubines or of public sinners, though the following conditions must be satisfied: a definitive commitment (which does not mean one that is indissoluble), the sole marriage, freedom of the spouses, acceptance of children . . . . In 1977 the International Theological Commission recognised that there could be a problem in regard to the validity of a sacramental marriage effected without any personal faith, but the only solution is the evangelisation of such candidates for marriage. As for baptised persons who would avoid even minimal reference to Christ (to God) and to the Church, they ought not to be admitted to the celebration of the sacrament of marriage. As far as other baptised persons are concerned, says John Paul II, the Church allows the celebration of marriage, even in the case of an imperfect disposition on the part of the partners. Therefore the Church would acknowledge a real (even if inchoate) sacramentality in various forms of conjugal relations from the moment of union granted, in addition to the above mentioned conditions, minimal publicity and faith (including possibly implicit faith). While refusing, in regard to baptised persons, to integrate any kind of conjugal relations into the sacramental reality (no one would gain anything from such confusions), doctrine refuses to identify the sacrament with a single model of marriage. It would recognise a *real though gradated sacramental reality* (inchoate in certain cases; 'fuller' in others) in various forms of conjugality.

From my point of view, it would then be necessary to speak of different ways of realising the sacramental dimension of marriage, or rather of distinguishing between *various degrees of sacramentality*. In any case, it is not the difference between sacramental and non-sacramental marriage that has to be indicated, but the differences between various ways in which married baptised persons can accord with the Church's intention and faith. In the end, as far as the content of marital commitment is concerned, we surely have to find a better way of articulating the demands of Christian marriage with those of faith. It is possible to work out one's choice and living of marriage 'in the Lord' only in faith in the love of God; that too demands a minimal relationship with the Church.

In the Church today the function of *matrimonial jurisprudence* (both on a rotal and on a diocesan level) is obviously becoming increasingly important, on condition of course that diocesan or regional bureaucracies have sufficient qualified people available. In spite of its abstract nature, any rule of law must necessarily apply to actual reality. *Therefore it has to be interpreted.* At the time of the 1917 Code, the almost exclusive method of interpretation was exegetical expertise. The Code was presumed to contain all necessary solutions. 'Do not venture outside the texts' was the principle applied. To be sure, they did not restrict themselves to a literal analysis of the law; the preparatory work on the law was consulted to discover the *mens legislatoris*, or recourse was had to legal tradition. In short, 'exegetes' thought they could answer all needs; in so doing, however, they failed to acknowledge the *desuetude of texts and the evolution of society.*

Admittedly these exegetical methods remain useful and necessary, inasmuch as the law corresponds to the real needs of communities. That is not to say that they do not become inadequate when the social reality no longer corresponds to the one obtaining when they were enacted. Then the need is felt for a *more dynamic interpretation*, whose intention would be no longer to look for what the legislator *had intended*, but rather what he *would have intended* given the new state of things, but taking into account, of course, the general spirit of the law (in order to avoid any arbitrary solution).[2]

In the Church the growing importance of jurisprudence also occurs within the context of a complex of ecclesial problems. It is a question of the 'vital relationship' which should obtain within the Church between the universal Church and the individual churches, between the given and the lived, between the general and abstract law and those whose mission is to apply the law.

More and more, therefore, jurisprudence is called on to assume the function of interpretation of the Code, which implies the function of *adaptation of the law to demands of evolving communities* (when a problem has not been foreseen by the legislator). Even if jurisprudence is not a source of the law in the strict sense, in the present canonical system, it nonetheless has a certain creative part to play (it is a derived source of the law). Congar recently emphasised the relevance of a trinitarian theology of the Church. A more acute awareness that the *entire ecclesial body is quickened by the Holy Spirit*, and that not only the universal Church but each individual church around its bishop is the temple of the Spirit, would provoke a more precise sense of the responsibility of regional and diocesan bureaucracies.

The real problem is as follows: *Are the official bodies capable of fulfilling their ministerial function*? Are they really acting in the service of the theologal life of Christians who have recourse to their ministry? 'The salvation of souls should always be the supreme law in the Church' (can. 1752). As for the judge, he should evaluate evidence in accordance with his conscience (can. 1608 par. 3). That is, matrimonial law does not primarily exist in the form of an abstract model which it is then enough to apply in pure and simple form. The historical and actual character of jurisprudence is not 'given' in advance. It is up to the official bodies to 'receive' it, to shape it, and to give it an appropriate embodiment in each age so that it can fulfil its mission, in obedience to the Spirit of Christ. The unity of jurisprudence in the Church is not the juridical or ideological uniformity of a totalitarian State. It is always something which has to be shaped or re-shaped. The unity is moving 'ahead' of us and demands a constant effort from everyone.

The legal innovations of the 1983 Code have been described on several occasions. The *new heads of nullity* for psychological reasons (absence of *discretio iudicii*, an inability to assume and carry out the essential obligations of marriage, the new interpretation of mistaken judgment of the quality of the individual . . .) encircle all the spiritual needs of numberous couples in a distressing situation to be answered. There is then a considerable temptation constantly to polish present jurisprudence and to continue adding to the already long list of heads under which nullity can be declared. There are, however, many canon lawyers who think that the time has come to *move beyond the system of declarations of nullity*. Does the concept of 'declaration of nullity' any longer correspond to the new conception of marriage, community of life and love? Is it possible to declare that a chunk of someone's life is null?

Several pastoral solutions have been proposed and tried out, but none of them has proved satisfactory and the need has been felt for ratification on a canonical level. The principle of indissolubility is safeguarded, the adherents of pastoral solutions suppose, and in practice pastors would prove flexible.

Here, finally, is a *short survey* of a few elements towards a solution of the problem as outlined.

—The discussions and colloquia on this topic have shown that if one *jettisons the philosophical, theological and historical discourse* relating to the entire complex of problems, harm is certainly done and the results are both banal and fruitless.

—*Matrimonial commitment (consensus)* is seen more and more as a *developing act* (and no longer as a mere occasion). The initial consent is the beginning of an interpersonal relationship which has to grow deeper day by day. The consistency of the relationship does not depend solely on the initial relationship, but also on various relations which may develop during the lived matrimonial state.

—Theologically speaking, it is the *living of marriage and not only the exchange of commitments* which is increasingly considered to be the sacramental sign of marriage.

—The indissoluble bond of marriage is not *an impersonal legal reality*, a bond which exists of itself, independently of the persons whom it unites.

—The new canonical procedure must very obviously take on a very marked *pastoral character*. It is a matter of casting off the legal rigour of a judicial procedure in favour of a simpler process which would be really in the service of the Word of God and of its beneficial action for human beings as they actually are.

—The procedure envisaged would eventuate *neither in a declaration of nullity nor a dissolution of marriage*. The official instance would confirm that this or that marriage contributed neither to the spiritual and human well-being of the partners nor to that of the community. This confirmation of non-arrival at the state of sufficient marital consistency could correspond canonically to the issue of a 'certificate of freedom to marry'. In the context of declarations of nullity, that might also mean: insufficient consent to a life lived in common. — Under the circumstances, it is certainly necessary to avoid both a *rendering banal of the act of marriage* (for instance, when divorce has been requested for far from weighty reasons, or without taking into account the family as constituted, or merely for personal convenience), and on the other hand a *desacralisation of official procedures* (we should not obscure the 'sacramental' nature of these proceedings; it is surely curious that in order to declare a sacramental marriage to be null we should choose above all specifically 'natural' and purely human motives).

—It is also important that we do not neglect the aspect of 'mercy, a Gift of

God', for which we should give thanks to God and which implies a commitment to conversion.

—New problems arise fro the *official bodies involved*. What pastoral initiatives are to accompany the notification of the final decision to interested persons and communities? What pastoral measures are required for preparation for a new marriage?

—'For us divorces do not primarily indicate some suppositious degree of moral weakness, but more generally the experience of a setback to a happy encounter, a breakdown in a communication insufficiently grounded in love'.[3]

Let us acknowledge the fact that the new Code has its troublesome aspects. But we must not forget that it is necessarily the expression of a situation which is both a culmination and a starting point. Our main hope is that this Code should not often remain a dead letter, as it may do if apostolic zeal and imagination are not put to work marking out new paths even within the very structure of the new norms.

Notes

1. E. Sullerot *Pour le meilleur et sans le pire* (Paris 1984).
2. J.-L. Aubert *Introduction au droit* (Paris 1984).
3. G. Defois *L'Occident en mal d'espoir* (1982) p. 93.

Libero Gerosa

Penal Law and Ecclesial Reality: the Applicability of the Penal Sanctions laid down in the New Code

1. THE CRITERION FOR MEASURING THE APPLICABILITY OF A PENAL SANCTION IN CANON LAW

IN THE actual life of the Church, on the pastoral level, much of the peal canon law codified in the *Codex Iuris Canonici* of 1917 had become *a dead letter* well before Vatican II. On the doctrinal level, however, the debate among canonists on the ecclesiological significance of the application of canonical punishments has never definitely been resolved. There are many reasons for this, of which it is worth examining at least two.

In the first place, the philosophy of law inspired by Christian thinking has repeatedly stated the possibility that *coercion may not necessarily belong to the formal notion of law*. This observation can be found already in so many words in St Thomas Aquinas, for whom the coercive element is not necessary *'ex se, sed posito alio'*.[1]

In the second place, the distinction made in the general theory of statute law,[2] between the *compulsoriness and the applicability of juridical norms*, is most applicable precisely to the law of the Church, in which concepts such as *ignorantia, epicheia,* or *aequitas canonica* still preserve their full normative force, without this derogating from the compulsoriness of canon law. This need to temper canon law to the person of the faithful is further strengthened, in the penal realm, by just the pastoral concern with which the Council of

Trent, inspired by St Paul (2 Tim. 4: 2), invited the bishops always to adopt coercive measures '*cum mansuetudine rigor, cum misercordia iudicium, cum lenitate severitas*' (1917, can. 2214, 2).

So both from the pastoral standpoint, and particularly from the doctrinal, it is more than legitimate to wonder whether the new '*De sanctionibus in Ecclesia*' will be able to be applied effectively and will command an understanding adherence in faith on the part of all the faithful. The criterion for measuring the applicability of canonical sanctions derives from their capacity for expressing, as comprehensibly as possible, the particularity of ecclesial juridical order, which, unlike that of the secular arm, derives not from the 'spontaneous dynamism of human society', but from the specific dynamism of grace, and can therefore only be known through faith.[3]

The question of the applicability of the penal sanctions decreed in the new Code therefore leads to the basic question, explored in its radical dimensions as part of the conflicts and tensions that emerged in the process of Church renewal initiated by Vatican II, concerning the coherence of the Church with its own sacramental structure and mission of salvation when it inflicts penalties on those who disobey its laws.

In other words, '*De sanctionibus in Ecclesia*' will be the more applicable in the present stage of Church life the more ecclesiastical legislators take account, in working out this new set of rules, of the importance given by the Council to the axiom that 'the act of faith is of its very nature a free act' (DH 10), precisely because not only theologians, but equally bishops, found it necessary to ask for a complete revision of the whole of Church law and especially for a drastic reduction in, or even total abolition of, penal canon law.[4]

2. THE CENSORING OF THE DOCTRINAL DEBATE ABOUT REFORM

During the process of revising the Church's Code, the '*Pontificia Commissio CIC Recognoscendo*' declared the idea of abolishing penal canon law to be absolutely unacceptable on the grounds that '*ius coactivum*' is proper to every '*societas perfecta*'.[5] In other words, this Commission, with no hesitation—and this in a climate of progressive 'democratisation' of Church structures, not to say even of radicalism in some quarters, that would tend to deny the very existence of authority in the Church—simply tells the canonists, and through them the faithful, that there is no change from the penal theory of the *Ius Publicum Ecclesiaticum*, which justifies the existence of coercive canonical power on purely sociological grounds. Using a natural law-based philosophical category, as such incapable of mediating a theological understanding of law in the Church, the defenders of the IPE justify the existence of coercive canonical power by 'deduction' and thereby end up reducing the Church to a mere natural law society.

Using this philosophical justification, the Pontifical Commission has taken a course which is difficult to accept if one takes account of the fact that the Council Fathers refused to include a systematic chapter on Church-State relations in the final text of *Lumen gentium*. In this proposed chapter, the nature of the Church was viewed under its aspect of juridically perfect society, and the effect was to show that such a description, at least on the dogmatic level, cannot be considered as being in the same league as images such as 'Body of Christ', 'People of God' or 'Sacrament of the world'.

The deep disquiet felt by theologians and canonists on the eve of the promulgation of the new Code is, therefore, more than understandable. Such philosophically-based justifications, like all *'a priori'* proofs, are just not enough. And it is not enough either to explain the refusal by the suggestion that an initial canon should set out positively the aims of penal canon law, simply because definitions are the task of doctrine and not of legislators.[6] In the present Church context, decisions of this nature look like taking the easy way out to a dangerous extent.[7]

Today, more than ever, *canonists have to show the theological bases and ecclesiological meaning of Church law* itself and, for their part, Church legislators have the duty to do everything possible to make every rule laid down in Church law somehow communicate these theological reasonings to the faithful. This is even more true of the sector of juridical Church order most questioned today: penal law. Failure to attend to this basic doctrinal and pastoral task means risking opening an unbridgeable gulf between law and sacrament.

It was most probably to avoid this danger that a request for the ecclesiological significance of canonical sanctions to be made plain formed the main content of the wish expressed by the special committee of the Canon Law Society of America, forwarded to the Holy See together with the official replies of the Committee of the American bishops' conference for Canonical Affairs.[8] How and to what extent does Book VI of the new Code take this basic wish into account?

3. THE AMBIGUITY OF THE NEW *'DE SANCTIONIBUS IN ECCLESIA'*

If the *guidelines on excommunication* set out in the new Code are compared with its *concept of punishment*, as expressed in '*De sanctionibus . . .* ', it is really very difficult to hide the fact that they differ widely from one another, and that there is therefore an *ambiguity* in the Church lawyers' reply to the insistent demand that the ecclesiological significance of the presence of penal sanctions in the Church's juridical order should be made clear.[9]

On the one hand, the new Code always imposes excommunication as a punishment *latae sententiae*, except in two cases: where this is seen as a possible aggravation, after interdiction and suspension inflicted *latae sententiae* (can. 1378, 3), and when the real crime is greater than the case in point (can. 1388, 2). Strictly speaking, excommunication can be sanctioned *latae sententiae* even in these two cases and then, given the gravity of both offences, the competent authority can declare it openly through a decree or sentence. These two exceptions merely serve to confirm the tendency of the new Code to consider excommunication normally as a penalty *latae sententiae*. In this way Church lawyers, in accordance with the principle that in canon law legal certainty can never prevail over objective and theological truth, can indicate, at least indirectly, that the canonical institution of *excommunicato* is, of its nature, a mere *declaratio*. A further proof of this is the fact that excommunication *latae sententiae* is upheld even in cases of so-called offences originating in apostasy, heresy and schism, which throws light on the theological bases of the *declaratory nature of excommunication*. This is not a punishment inflicted by the will of the ecclesiastical authorities, but rather the confirmation of an existing situation: that of non-communion, in which the subject has placed himself through his anti-Church attitude. John Paul II expressed himself in this sense in his first address to the Rota: ' . . . the penalty imposed by the ecclesiastical authorities (but which is really a recognition of a situation in which the subject has placed himself) is seen . . ..as an instrument of communion'.[10] In other words, it is not the ecclesiastical authority that creates the situation of break in *communio* through its intervention; it merely recognises it and eventually declares it so that it becomes known to the person concerned and to the whole Church.

On the other hand, the concept of canonical punishment underlying the new Code is substantially the same as that found in the section '*De delictis et poenis*' of the 1917 Code, as can be seen from canons 1311, 1312, 1341 and 1399.

Particularly in canon 1341, where the spirit of the Church's new penal code is '*maxime perfusus*', this '*in recto*' invites the ordinary to inflict or declare a canonical censure only after having confirmed the failure of all other methods dictated by pastoral care, while '*oblique*' affirms that '*reparatio scandalum*', '*restitutio justitiam*' and '*emendatio rerum*' are the ends of all ecclesiastical penalties, exactly as in the 1917 Code, the authors of which had appropriated the mixed penal theories (particularly that of juridical tutelage) worked out for the most part by Catholic penalists of the late nineteenth century and then systematically incorporated into the canonical legislation of the IPE.[11] Now, can this concept of punishment realistically be applied to excommunication, which the new Code considers a mere declaration?

The reply cannot be other than negative if one considers the main effect of excommunication, which consists in the ban laid on the excommunicated person from free access to the sacrament of penance. Indeed, the need to obtain prior and *in foro externo* 'legitimate absolution' of the excommunication is not a true and proper *retributio*. Its end is neither *reparatio scandalum* nor *restitutio iustitiam*, but rather safeguarding *communio* through the full amendment of the subject, which makes such a ban an added difficulty in the way of rendering his desire for reconciliation with the Church credible. So, the healing character of the excommunication does not qualify the ban as an *effectum poenale* of the excommunication, but rather as a penance, or perhaps an *'aggravatio penitentiae'*, that is a penance held over in anticipation on the analogy of what happened before the separation of the sacrament of penance from penal canon law.

This is not a very bold hypothesis if it is seen in the light of what might be taken as the key to a reading of '*De sanctionibus in Ecclesia',* canon 1344, according to which the ecclesiastical judge, even when the law uses preceptive terms, can substitute a *poenitentia* for the penalty, even though this would not form part of *'poenae strictae dictae'*. History as well as systematic theology would point to the legitimacy of this, since there is a clear basic parallel between the ecclesiastical juridical obligation to require the *legitima absolutio* of the excommunication and the dogmatic need for recourse to the sacrament of penance once the subject who is conscious of having committed a grave sin wants to return to full communion with God and the Church. Finally, the hypothesis is confirmed by the tendency of the new Code to multiply the 'extraordinary circumstances' in which the penitent criminal can avoid, even when not on the point of death, recourse to the competent superior and can receive absolution from excommunication *latae sententiae 'in foro interno sacramentali'*.[12]

This last observation helps to make the point that, since the judgement that makes up *excommunicatio* is not constitutive but declaratory, the re-establishment of full communion depends above all on the freedom of the person excommunicated. Indeed, as soon as he rescinds his *contumacia,* he enjoys the so-called *'ius ad absolutionem'* and then the *'remissio poenae'* (consisting in another judgement of a declaratory nature which opens the way to full reconciliation with God and the Church, effected through sacramental absolution) cannot be refused him by the proper Church authority (can. 1358, 1).

Excommunication, the penalty that typifies the juridical order of the Church, is therefore far from exemplifying the Code's concept of punishment, as expressed in particular in canon 1341. The less so, being based on a declaratory judgement, can it be considered a 'must be', that is, as a juridical and moral necessity in the same way that a civil penalty is by virtue of its essentially coercive and retributive nature, needing therefore always to be applied and executed *'propter maleficium'*. So, the new juridical order of the Church, by keeping excommunication *latae sententiae*—a peculiarly ecclesial sentence—in force, and by stressing its basically declaratory nature, not just the healing character of its main juridical effect, clearly shows how this *type of canonical sanction fails to correspond to the Code's overall concept of punishment.* Faced with this divergence, there is no denying the existence of a *double spirit* within *De sanctionibus in Ecclesia.*

One side, the more theological, of this spirit, viewing excommunication as a sanction normally applied *latae sententiae* by virtue of its declaratory nature, adequately expresses the ecclesiology of Vatican II, particularly the teaching of LG 14, 2 concerning the incidence of grave sin on 'full incorporation', with its logical consequence of the parallel between self-exclusion from ecclesial communion, which is what excommunication consists of, and *exclusio* from the Eucharist broght about by grave sin.[13]

Its *second, more positivist, side* reveals first and foremost, on the level of terminology and basic penal law, a strict dependence on the cultural stamp and juridical methodology of the old Code and, in the final analysis, of the *Ius Publicum Ecclesiaticum.* These penal principles inherited from the 1917 Code cannot, however, be applied to the most typical sanction of those known to canon law. This observation, while on one hand confirming once again the prevalence of one sort of general theory of law in the ecclesiology of Vatican II,[14] on the other hand places a huge question mark over all the new rules governing canonical sanctions, since it brings us right up against the unresolved basic problem: Are penal sanctions really applicable in the Church?

In other words, the fact that the *two sides of the spirit are not integrated but exist alongside each other,* allows the antinomy between *coactio* and *libera fides* to re-emerge in the new Code. This dualism, in the ecclesial understanding of the post-conciliar period, looks increasingly like the tip of an iceberg, whose submerged base is the more *radical opposition between law and charity, law and sacrament.*

This has one effect of preventing *De sanctionibus*... from applying its greatest virtue on the pastoral level: its brevity—89 canons as opposed to 320 in the *De delictis et poenibus* of the old Code. It has another, in that such dualism makes the new codification call back into question the one question that there seemed no escape from on the eve of the reform: the net separation between *foro externo* and *foro interno*, which was considered the indispensible condition for allowing penal law full citizenship in the body of canon law, expressed in the axiom, *'in solo foro externo irrogatur et remittantur'*.[15]

Those who were convinced that the preparation of a new juridical order based on the sacramental structure of the Church was a lengthy task have, therefore, had their fears that this was a wasted opportunity confirmed.[16]

HOW TO SALVAGE THIS WASTED OPPORTUNITY ON THE DOCTRINAL LEVEL?

If we are to develop a *concept of canonical sanctionary discipline that does not diverge structurally from the notion of the Church as sacrament of salvation*, canonists must first compare canonical sanctions with the general theory of penal and disciplinary sanctions as worked out by contemporary penal law, working within a rigorous methodology, one that is capable of accepting the comparison without however seeing secular law as the *analogatum princeps*, since both canon law and secular law are analogous realisations of the primordial notion of law.

The first conclusion canonists would draw from this work is undoubtedly that canonical sanctions are not 'punishments'. Indeed, if excommunication cannot be considered a punishment, even in an analogous sense, by the same token the other two ecclesiastical censures, interdiction and suspension, which have to be set aside as soon as the delinquent abjures his *contumacia* (can. 1358, 1), are not punishments either, since the remission of punishment is tied to the principle of *expiatio*. The so-called *'poenae expiatoriae'* are directly aimed at this, but this is not sufficient to define them either as true and proper punishments. Indeed, canon law, dealing with *expiatio* as the normal mode of cessation of these sanctions, also knows a *'modus extraordinarius'* for their remission: *dispensatio,* which is an *'actus gratiae'* of the competent authority, which can therefore act either *'ex iustitiae'* or purely *'ex mera indulgentia'*.[17] In inflicting such canonical punishments, the Church does not forget either the healing effect of correction, nor the need to correct with charity. Their aim therefore is not solely expiation of the crime, nor is their retributive nature wholly divorced from any connection with the penitential discipline of the Church.

Expiatory penalties, which unlike excommunication could as well not exist, yet have a further formal aspect in common with the canonical institution of excommunication: they too can be declared or drawn up *'per modum precepti extra iudicium'*.[18] So both censures and expiatory penalties escape from rigorous application of the principle *'nulla poena sine processu'*, which no system of civil penal law can ever renounce. The possibility of their being applied by administrative means suggests that both expiatory penalties and disciplinary measures can be considered *sui generis*, for at least two reasons.

The first is that so-called 'expiatory penalties' have no direct effect on reception of the sacraments, but only on their administration. They are therefore normally applied only to clergy, religious or lay people who exercise a particular ecclesial ministry; always, then, in cases where there is a clear analogy with the special juridical relationship that exists between the State and its public servants.

The second is that the various prohibitions and privations set out in canon 1336, 1 as 'expiatory penalties', can properly be applied by the ecclesiastical authority only after proving the unsuitability of the subject to take up or continue to fulfil the obligations belonging to a particular ecclesial ministry. In such cases the intervention of the ecclesiastical authority will be dicated in the first place by reasons of opportunity which, as such, take no account of the question of guilt, which is nevertheless basic to any decision on criminal responsiblity.

The very fact that such a hypothesis can validly be formulated amply justifies the need to reconsider more attentively the suggestion made by Peter Huizing, at the beginning of the reform process, in the pages of *Concilium*,[19] that the *concept of 'penal law' should be dropped in favour of that of 'disciplinary order' of the Church*, since all canonical sanctions are directed primarily to the defence of the community and not 'against' an individual, as civil penalties are. The aim of canonical sanctions is not to punish an individual or imbue him with coercive measures for his conversion; their purpose is rather to maintain the purity of the Church's preaching and to bear witness to its faith. Canonical sanctions, Huizing concludes, are therefore not punishments but disciplinary sanctions.

This approach leaves several problems unresolved: for example one would need to establish how far it is possible to introduce such a clear distinction between public and private into Church law. One would also need to ask if excommunication, always the exemplar of Church sanctions, could be qualified among the so-called disciplinary sanctions. There are two basic reasons why it cannot.

In the first place, to be able to incur excommunication, the faithful do not need to be invested with special obligations deriving from the exercise of a particular ecclesial ministry. In the second, because for excommunication to apply there must always be intentional elements present in the anti-Church attitude of the subject, elements that prevent responsibility for such an attitude being deduced solely from the unsuitability of the subject or from negligence, as sometimes happens in disciplinary matters.

The equal weight given to the two aspects, penal and disciplinary, by the peculiar theological nature of excommunication, guarantees a specific originality to the whole sanctionary system of the Church. This system should be seen for what it is in fact, in the light of its essential relationship with the sacrament of penance: a system of penances of a pastoral-disciplinary nature.[20] This distinction is of no little importance. Indeed, unlike punishment, *poenitentia* always presupposes a minimum of good disposition on the part of the penitent. For this reason, *poenitentia*, together with '*remedia poenalia*, even when applied '*in foro externo*' (can. 1340, 1), does not formally belong to the '*poenae strictae dictae*'.

Consequently, the Church's various sanctions could basically be considered as a special category of so-called '*poenitentiae canonicae*'. Placing them in a distinct category like this, while connecting them with the sacrament of penance, would have given more emphasis to the penitential-pastoral nature of all canonical sanctions and would perhaps have enabled *De sanctionibus in Ecclesia* to overcome the real difficulties that remain in the way of its becoming an effective future instrument in restoring credibility to the whole question of canonical discipline.

Translated by Paul Burns

Notes

1. *De veritate* 23, 4 ad 1.
2. See A. Levi *Teoria generale del diritto* (Padua 1967) pp. 160–73.
3. On the significance of this methodological principle for the whole of canon law, see E. Corecco *Theologie des Kirchenrechts. Methodologische Ansätze* (Trier 1980) pp. 79–107.
4. This is one of the arguments that provoked the most numerous interventions from the bishops at the 1967 Synod.
5. See *Communicationes* 1 (1969) pp. 84–5.
6. See *ibid.* 8 (1976) pp. 166–7.
7. This is the verdict arrived at by F. Nigro in 'Le sanzioni della Chiesa come tutela della comunione ecclesiale' in *La nuova legislazione canonica* (Rome 1983) pp. 423-66, esp. 438.

8. See J. Provost, 'Reactions to the Proposal for a New Penal Code', which was published in all the language editions except English, since the English-language edition was interrupted for two years of this time.

9. This paragraph summarises the main contents of the communication to the Fifth International Congress of Canon Law (Ottawa, 16–19 Aug. 1984).

10. AAS 71 (1979) p. 415.

11. For a full analysis of the part played by these theories in the 1917 Code, see L. Gerosa *La scomunica è una pena?* (Fribourg 1984).

12. See canons 1352, 1; 1355, 2; 1356, 2 and 1357, 1.

13. On this point see H. Müller 'Zugehörigkeit zur Kirche als Problem der Nuekodifikation des canonischen Rechts' in *ÖAfKR* 28 (1977) 81–98; L. Gerosa 'Ist der Kirchenbann eine Strafe?' in *AfKKR* (1985).

14. See J. Provost, 'The R evised Code of Canon Law: Expectations and Results' in *Concilium* 147 (7/1981) 4 pp. 3–9; and the article by E. Corecco in the present issue.

15. De Paolis himself, who upheld the introduction of this principle into Church law, is forced to admit that the new Code does not resolve the question but rather complicates it. See V. de Paolis 'Il Libro VI' in *Il nuovo CIC. Studi* (Turin 1985) p. 265.

16. See 'The revised Code of Canon Law: A Misled Opportunity?' ed. P. Huizing and K. Wolf, *Concilium* 147 (7/1981).

17. See canons 2289 and 2290 of the 1917 Code and the commentary by G. Michels *De delictis et poenis* (Paris 1961) II p. 430.

18. See A. Arza *De poenis infligendis via administrativa: Questioni attuali di Diritto Canonico* (Rome 1955) pp. 457–76.

19. P. Huizing 'Crime and Punishment in the Church' in *Concilium* 8, 3 (1967).

20. See A. Arza 'Derecho penal en la Iglesia' in *Investigationes Theologicocanonicae* (Rome 1978) pp. 15–38, esp. 34–38.

John Huels

Parish Life and The New Code

THE PARISH is most probably the most important level of the Church's life because for most people it is there that the Church exists—the community gathers for worship; its communion with the larger diocesan and universal Church is symbolised and effected; its outreach and witness to the world is inspired and begun. Since the parish is so vital to the Church, it is imperative that canon law support parish life and facilitate its ministry in keeping with the diverse needs of the local churches around the world. The purpose of this article is to see how successfully the 1983 revision of the Code of Canon Law has accomplished this goal. Primarily the discussion will be limited to a survey of some key changes in the section on parishes in the code (canons 515–552) but, since many areas of the law affect parish life, certain problems connected with some of these other areas will also be briefly considered.

Some immediately evident changes in the revised code concern the structuring and title of the chapter on parishes and the very notion of what a parish is. The 1917 code had two chapters, one on pastors and one on parochial vicars, a division that was appropriate to the structure of Book II entitled *De personis* ('Persons'), the section of that code in which these two chapters were situated; however, the parish itself was not treated as a separate entity. The 1917 code considered the parish as a territorial section of the diocese to which a pastor was assigned for the care of souls, and also a benefice for the financial support of the pastor.[1] The emphasis of the former law was on the rights and duties of the pastor; the parishioners were referred to only indirectly and seen as the passive subjects of the care of souls with no recognition by the law of their having any active role in the functioning of the parish.

In comparing the law of the revised Code with the former Code on the subject of parishes, one notices a wholly different approach. The revised Code has only one chapter entitled 'Parishes, Pastors, and Parochial Vicars', thus *placing priority on the parish community itself before treating the pastor.* The initial canon 451 in the chapter on pastors of the 1917 Code presented a definition of a pastor; the initial canon 515 of the corresponding chapter of the revised code defines a parish instead. The new Code defines a parish as 'a definite community of the faithful (*christifideles*) established on a stable basis within a particular church. The new law views the parish as fundamentally a community of believers, a description faithful to the notion of parish in Vatican II[2] and to the system of the revised Code's second book—no longer called simply 'Persons' but given the biblically and theologically rich title, 'The People of God'. The notion of the parish as a community is also intrinsic to the new definition of a pastor found in canon 519 which states in part that the pastor exercises his duties for his community in cooperation with other presbyters or deacons and with laypersons.

Not only is the parish defined theoretically as a community of the faithful, but several new canons lay the juridical foundation for an *active share by deacons and laypersons in the financial administration and pastoral leadership of the parish,* including provisions for parish pastoral councils and finance councils and for administrators of priestless parishes. Concerning the *parish pastoral council,* the revised law leaves it to the diocesan bishop, after consulting the presbyteral council, to determine whether a parish council is to be established in each parish of the diocese (can. 536). This canon states that the parish council, presided over by the pastor, is composed of members of the faithful and others who have an office of pastoral care in the parish, and their task is to assist the pastor in fostering pastoral activity. The council has only consultative vote and is governed by norms determined by the diocesan bishop.

The Code has been criticised by some for not mandating parish councils universally or for not taking at least a more positive approach to them;[3] another critique holds that it would have been preferable had the code said nothing at all about the council to allow time for the body to develop and mature without legal restrictions such as the merely consultative vote. According to this view, the Code portrays the role of the parish council as only to serve the pastor; thus lay leadership and initiative would have had more freedom to develop in various ways if the Code had remained silent on the issue.[4] On the other hand, it is conceivable that if there were no mention of the parish council in the Code some bishops might see little reason for introducing it in their dioceses. Furthermore, by allowing the bishops to decide whether to have parish councils and by requiring them to consult the presbyteral council, the conciliar values of subsidiarity and collegiality are upheld. A greater flexibility is also accorded to the local churches to meet the needs and circumstances of diverse places, as, for example, in primitive societies which may not be ready for parish councils. Even in some places in developed countries experiences with parish councils have not always been positive. For this reason it is not enough for the bishop simply to mandate the council; he must see to it that clergy and lay leaders have a suitable formation to prepare them for the dynamics, responsibilities, and realistic objectives of council membership.

The *parish finance council* is a new juridical structure introduced by the revised Code (can. 537) that will surely increase lay involvement and leadership in the parish and at the same time make the ordained leadership more accountable. Every parish is required to have a finance council made up of members of the faithful whose purpose is to assist the pastor in the financial administration of the parish. In contrast to the parish council, the finance council is not optional according to the discretion of the bishop but is mandated by the universal law. However, in keeping with the principle of subsidiarity, the bishop is given the competence to enact norms governing the composition and responsibilities of the body; this also allows flexibility for the varying needs and circumstances of local churches.

The finance council is intended to be a consultive body primarily responsible to the pastor who has the legal authority to represent the parish in all juridic affairs (can. 532). Although it lacks decision-making power as a general rule, the diocesan bishop could establish instances where the council's deliberative vote would be necessary, such as approving the annual budget, exceeding the limits set for extraordinary expenditures, establishing salaries for lay employees not subject to diocesan norms, and similar cases.

The benefits of a finance council are apparent. The pastor frequently is not as proficient in financial matters as some lay parishioners are, and their advice on and oversight of parish finances can help the pastor with budgets, investments, reports and the like, which not only promotes fiscal responsibility and accountability but also frees the pastor for other tasks.

Some confusion has been created in certain areas about the relationship of the finance council to the parish council. Before the revised code took effect, many parish councils were entrusted with the responsibilities which the Code has given to the finance council. Although the finance council is clearly envisioned as an entity distinct from the parish council, there is nothing in the law to prevent the diocesan bishop from permitting or requiring that the finance council be accountable to or even being a part of or equated with the parish council. The code leaves all such details to the judgment of the bishop.

Another innovation in the Code that certainly advances the role of non-priests in the leadership of the parish is the provision for a *deacon, layperson, or community of persons to share in the pastoral care of a parish when there is a scarcity of priests* (can. 517, §2). In some areas of the world this office is commonly called the 'administrator', but the Code does not have a name for it. Whenever such an administrator is placed in charge of a parish, the law states that the bishop must appoint a priest as pastor to supervise the pastoral care of the parish. The typical situation would be the parish without a resident pastor but with a priest who visits periodically to celebrate the sacraments and to supervise pastoral care as may be needed. The priest in question can be the pastor of one or more neighbouring parishes, as permitted by canon 526, §1, or any other priest appointed by the bishop. The law is quite flexible and open-ended, leaving it to the bishop to determine particular matters, such as what constitutes a scarcity of priests, the qualifications of the office of administrator, the rights and duties pertaining to the office, and the relationship of the administrator to parishioners and pastor.

Underlying all the innovations in the law on parishes discussed so far have been *certain values such as fidelity to Vatican II ecclesiology, subsidiarity, flexibility, and a broader participation by non-priests in parish leadership.* Some of these and other values, such as *collegiality*, can also be discerned in other changes in the law, including provisions for team ministry, a fixed term of office for pastors, and mandatory retirement of pastors.

In his apostolic constitution promulgating the revised Code, Pope John Paul II stated that the new law was drafted in an 'outstandingly *collegial* spirit' and it reflects collegiality in 'the very substance of the laws enacted'.[5] The provision for a team ministry, or co-pastorate, is an example of how the Code has promoted the value of collegiality, in so far as team ministry can be viewed as a form of presbyteral collegiality rooted historically in the ancient *presbyterium* gathered around the bishop.[6] Canon 517, § 1 states that, when circumstances require it, the pastoral care of a parish or of several parishes together can be entrusted to a team of several priests *in solidum*, that is, each priest on the team has all the ordinary powers and obligations of pastor.[7] All team members equally share in the office of pastor; however, one of the priests serves as moderator to direct their combined activity and answer for it to the bishop in keeping with the general rule that there be only one pastor or one moderator for each parish (can. 526, §2). Once again one sees a great deal of flexibility in the law; he bishop is free to decide what circumstances may require team ministry, such as the good of the priests themselves and/or the parish or parishes served by them.

The values of subsidiarity and flexibility are also seen in the provision of canon 522 allowing the diocesan bishop, in regions where the episcopal conference has given its approval, *to appoint pastors for a fixed term*. In such regions the bishop is completely free to use this provision or not, depending on how he views local needs and circumstances. This is a significant departure from past law; never before has the general law allowed limits to be set on the term of the pastor's office,[8] although in recent years an indult was obtainable for this purpose. The ideal of the former law was stability in the pastoral office since the parish was viewed as a benefice for the support of the pastor, and the law protected this stability to guarantee the livelihood of priests. Although stability in office is still a value and is stated as such in canon 522, the new law, by making possible a fixed term of office, implicitly recognises in this practice certain advantages for both pastor and parish. The parish, for example, can experience a greater variety of pastoral styles with greater frequency, and it enjoys a greater sense of stability in knowing when the pastor will be succeeded. This latter can be especially advantageous to the parish that has an incompetent or unpopular pastor because it is offered the prospect of a replacement at a definite point in the future. For the pastor himself a limited term can lessen the burdens of the pastorate, facilitate a transition from a difficult situation, prevent personal stagnation, and provide stimulation and job satisfaction.[9] Of course, there can also be certain disadvantages to the fixed term, notably the case when a parish loses a very likeable and competent pastor and receives someone less effective as his successor.

Somewhat related to the issue of a fixed term of office is the new requirement of canon 538, §3 that the pastor, on completing his 75th year of age, is to submit his *resignation* to the diocesan bishop. Once again the law is flexible and allows the bishop to accept or defer the resignation. This is the first time in history that provision is made by universal law for mandatory retirement from the pastoral office.[10] One can readily see that some of the same advantages in having a fixed term of office are relevant also to the retirement of pastors.

In general, the innovations in the law on parishes in the revised Code indicate that *its drafters were successful, both theoretically and in practice, in implementing the principles that guided the reform of the Code as a whole.*[11] The canons on parishes reflect a number of important ecclesiological principles emphasised at Vatican II, including subsidiarity, collegiality, the importance of the diocesan bishop and the local church community, and the active role of the layperson in Church life. The section on parishes in the revised Code is also quite acceptable from a practical perspective. It makes realistic provision for the Church of the future that will have fewer priests to staff parishes. It shows great flexibility in permitting local adaptations and specific determinations of the various parish structures, and in some cases making them optional. Such provisions as those for team ministry, parish pastoral and finance councils, and non-priests as administrators suggest a sensitivity in this section of the Code to post-conciliar developments and the needs and objectives of contemporary parish life.

This is not to say that everything in the section on parishes is perfect. Law follows life and therefore is always in need of reform. One criticism made about this section of the Code is its lack of attention to the *role of deacon in the parish*.[12] It is true that deacons are scarcely mentioned in the law on parishes, but that may be all for the better. As a general rule it is preferable for the universal law to say too little rather than too much on any matter, especially regarding something as new to the Church today as the restored permanent diaconate. The best code for a universal Church is one which establishes general principles and essential norms while allowing the particular churches to specify the details. The Code apparently is following this principle in regard to the role of deacons in the parish as well as other new developments in parish life, such as the division of parishes in some areas of the world into 'base communities'.[13]

One area in which the section on parishes in the revised Code has failed to integrate contempoarary theological understandings is its continued requirement of the *Missa pro populo*, the law of canon 534 obliging the pastor to celebrate the Eucharist for the intention of his parishioners on every Sunday and holy day of obligation. According to M. F. Mannion, 'the theology and practice of the ancient liturgical tradition, as well as the emerging liturgical praxis, hold that the Mass is always and of necessity *pro populo*, indeed, more fundamentally, *ex populo*'.[14] The whole thrust of the modern liturgical reform has been to promote the active participation of the faithful in the liturgy. The obligation of the *Missa pro populo* suggests, on the contrary, that the pastor's mere intention for his parishioners at Mass is more significant than his actively celebrating with them.

Although the requirement of the *Missa pro populo* is given in the section on parishes, it is based on the theology behind the *Mass offering (stipend) system* regulated in canons 945-958 in the section on the Eurharist. As such, the continued requirement of the *Miss pro populo* is more the failure of the Church's sacramental law to keep pace with current theology than its law on parishes.

Thus, while the Code's section on parishes is generally quite good, other parts of the Code which have a great affect on parish life are not always as adequate. Since space does not permit an examination in detail of these areas, it will have to suffice to mention a few issues without developing them as fully as may be desirable.

A major problem for parish ministry is the *shortage of priests around the world*, and it is well known that this shortage is caused to a great extent by the canonical requirement of mandatory celibacy (can. 277). The consequences of the priest shortage include 'an even closer identification of clergy with sacramental ministry, a less sacramentally focussed and more Word-focussed parish life, further pressures for the ordination of women and married people, and some depreciation of the sacerdotal role in parish life'.[15] The revised Code reflects an awareness of this problem by allowing deacons and lay people to assume many of the roles and offices formerly restricted to priests, including, as seen   above, serving as administrators of priestless parishes. Another example of the Code's attentiveness to the problem is seen in canon 1248, §2 in which the obligation to participate in the Mass on Sundays and holy days is mitigated when the celebration of the Eucharist is impossible as a result of the lack of a priest or for some other grave cause. In this case the law recommends that the faithful take part in the liturgy of the Word in the parish church or other sacred place, or spend an appropriate amount of time praying personally or as a family or in groups of families. While this is a realistic and laudable provision, it raises the question of the centrality of the sacraments, especially the Sunday Eucharist, in the Church's life. In so far as celibacy is a principal reason for the shortage of priests, it is not difficult to imagine that some will conclude that the preservation of compulsory priestly celibacy is more important to the legislator than the weekly celebration of the Eucharist in the local parish community.

A second problem that canon law creates for pastoral ministry is its *complexity and detail*. This is especially true of the law governing the discipline of the sacraments. The complicated marriage law is the outstanding example, but there are many others: the various conditions for the administration of certain sacraments to non-Catholic Christians (can. 844); the numerous restrictions on the celebration of penance with general absolution (canons 961–963); the detailed regulations governing Mass offerings (canons 945–958); the issue of the application of canon 144 to the sacraments of confirmation, penance, and marriage whereby the Church supplies the faculty lacking by the minister to preside at these three sacraments in cases of error that is common in fact or in law or in positive and probable doubt of law or fact. Another very complicated matter for the typical priest in the parish is the issue of penal law and its relationship to the sacrament of penance. One need only look at canons 1321–1329 to see how difficult it must be for a confessor to determine who has truly incurred an automatic (*latae sententiae*) penalty because there are so many criteria to keep in mind. Moreover, the procedure of canon 1357 for remitting the penalty by the confessor in the internal sacramental forum is itself needlessly complicated and dubiously effective.

The many legitimate demands made on seminary curricula today along with the expanded responsibilities of pastoral ministry necessarily result in a diminishment of the role of canon law in the preparation and apostolate of the parish priest. As a result, parish priests often no longer have the knowledge of canon law they once had; and it can be expected that permanent deacons and lay leaders have even less. As the priest shortage continues to worsen, the Church can anticipate increasing problems, indeed, even abuses, that result from the lack of training or sufficient memory needed to apply the complex legal system that regulates the sacraments.

Notes

1. P.G. Marcuzzi Verso una nuova definizione giuridica di parrochia' *Salesianum* 43 (1981) 833.

2. *Sacrosanctum Concilium*, 42; *Christus Dominus*, 30; *Lumen gentium*, 28. See F. Coccopalmerio 'Quaedam de conceptu paroeciae iuxta doctrinam Vaticani II' *Periodica* 70 (1981) 119–140.

3. See, e.g., J. Lynch 'The Parochial Ministry in the New Code of Canon Law' *The Jurist* 42 (1982) 401–402.

4. R. Page 'The Parish Council' *Proceedings of the Canon Law Society of America* 43 (1981) 45–61.

5. *Sacrae disciplinae leges* Jan. 25 (1983) *Acta Apostolicae Sedis* 75, Pars II (1983) viii.

6. J. Janicki in *The Code of Canon Law: A Text and Commentary* ed. J. Coriden, T. Green, and D. Heintschel (New York/Mahwah 1985) at p. 417.

7. Canons 542–545. See J.C. Perisset 'De applicatione conceptus "in solidum" ad novam figuram officii parochi' *Periodica* 73 (1984) 191–202.

8. Janicki, the article cited in note 6, ct p. 422.

9. *Ibid.*, 423; see also *idem*. 'Limited Term of Office and Retirement' *Proceedings of the Canon Law Society of America* 41 (1979) 42–45.

10. Lynch, the article cited in note 3, 407. The 1966 apostolic letter of Paul VI, *Ecclesiae Sanctae*, I, n. 20 requested *voluntary* retirement.

11. *Communicationes* 1 (1969) 77–85.

12. See the position of the canon law faculty of The Catholic University of America cited in Lynch, the article cited in note 3, 391, and that of the Canon Law Society of America cited in T. Green 'Critical Reflections on the Schema on the People of God *Studia Canonica* 14 (1980) 306–307.

13. See H. Hack 'Die Pfarrei' in *Handbuch des katholischen Kirchenrechts* ed. J. Listl, H. Müller, and H. Schmitz, (Regensburg, 1983) at p. 391.

14. M.F. Mannion 'Stipends and Eucharistic Praxis' *Worship* 57 (1983) 212–213.

15. *Parish Life in the United States: Final Report to the Bishops of the U.S. by the Parish Project*, Washington, D.C., U.S. Catholic Conference, 1983, 73. See also the Notre Dame Study of Catholic Parish Life, Report no. 2, Notre Dame, Indiana, Feb., 1985, 5.

Elizabeth McDonough

Women and the New Church Law

OBJECTIVELY SPEAKING *the new Church law places women in an enhanced juridic condition in comparison to the former code.* Scholarly studies of the 1917 code demonstrate that it viewed women as (1) functionally subordinate, (2) morally sinful and seductive, (3) intellectually inferior, and (4) emotionally unstable.[1] For the most part law flows from and follows life; it does not dictate or create reality. Thus it should be no surprise that numerous studies also indicate that this unequal canonical treatment of women was significantly influenced by former philosophical and theological perspectives expressed in particular historical and political circumstances.[2] Ecclesial documents of the past quarter century manifest an understanding of women that differs somewhat, and in a rather positive manner, from the view of former perspectives and circumstances. This newer ecclesial understanding perceives women as (1) equal in dignity to men with whom they share complementarity, (2) inherently good and redeemed by Christ although participating with men in the sinfulness of the human condition, and (3) enjoying intellect, judgment, initiative and responsibility for social and ecclesial endeavours along with men. With rare exception it is this newer understanding of women that is incorporated into the canons of the 1983 Code.

The positive adjustment of the juridic condition of women in the new law is also partially a consequence of the *enhanced position of the laity* in various aspects of ecclesial structure and functioning. This is a direct result of Vatican Council II. Following the lead of the Council, the Code Commission in its sixth principle for revision announced its desire to identify a common juridic Christian status for all the baptised. In keeping with this principle, when the 1983 code makes no specification regarding persons in particular canons, terms such as *laici* and *christifideles* are understood to include both women and men. Similarly, although the phrase is taken *verbatim* from 1917 Code canon 490 §2, the new Code canon 606 legislates equivalent application for women and men of all the canons on consecrated life unless the words or the matter involved indicate otherise.

When discussing the enhanced legal position of the laity and the more positive juridic condition of women, it is helpful to be aware of pertinent 1983 Code canons and the 1917 Code canons to which they correspond. A partial sequential list of these is contained in Table I.[3] In order to facilitate consideration, these canons can be conveniently divided into those which alter the condition of the laity in general and those which affect women in particular.

1. WOMEN AS LAITY

Many legal positions and numerous affirmed rights are new to the 1983 Code. Lay persons, whether women or men, may hold these positions d possess these rights. Some of the new positions which are open to qualified laity include those of diocesan finance officer (can. 494 §1), membership on the parish finance council (can. 537) and membership on the diocesan or parish pastoral councils (canons 512 §1, 536 §1). Various rights now affirmed for women and men in the Church include those of announcing the Good News (canons 211, 225), promoting apostolic action (can. 216), forming associations (can. 215), freely choosing one's state in life (can. 219), studying sacred disciplines (can. 229) and receiving appropriate remuneration for their work (can. 231).

Several roles and functions which are not new within Church structures, but which were formerly restricted to clerics, are now also areas of responsibility open to members of the laity. Adhering to the norms of the new Code, women and men can cooperate in the exercise of the power of governance (can. 129 §2), can be assumed to certain ecclesiastical offices and *munera* (canons 145, 228 §1), can serve as delegates or observers for the Apostolic See (can. 363 §2) and can participate in particular councils (can. 463). With certain restrictions for offices requiring the power of governance (can. 274 §1),[4] the new Code allows women and men to fulfill the offices of chancellor (can. 482

Table I: CHANGES IN THE LEGAL POSITION OF LAITY AND OF WOMEN

1983 code canons	1917 code canons
104	93§1
112 2	98§4
129§2	118
145§1	145§1
215	
228	118; 145§1
230§2,3	813§2
277§2	133
307§1	709§2
317§2	712§3
363§2	265; 269
463§1 5,9, §2	282§3; 286§4; 358; 360§1
482§1	372§1
492§1	1520§1
494§1	
512§1	
517§2	
536§1	
537	
592§1	510; 499§2; 517
625	506
630§3	520–527
636	533§1
637	535§§1,2
645	544§§2,7; 547§§1,3; 549
641; 656; 658	522§2
665	607; 645§2
667	598–604; 1264§2; 2342
766	1342§1
830§1	1393§1
910	845
861§2	742§2
964§3	910§1
1067	1020§2
1112	1096§1
1115	1097§2; 1109§2
1148§1	1125
1168	1146
1177	1229§2
1279§2	1521§1
1323–1324	2218§1
1702	1979–1981
1421§2	1574
1424	1575
1428§2	1581
1435	1589§1

§1), censor (can. 830 §1), judge in a collegiate tribunal (can. 1421 §2), assessor (can. 1421), auditor (can. 1428 §2) and defender of the bond or promoter of justice (can. 1435).

Numerous liturgical ministries and responsibilities which were formerly restricted to clerics now also fall within the competence of the laity who may perform them according to the norms of the new Code. Among other functions, women and men are permitted to exercise the ministries of lector, commentator and cantor (can. 230 § 2), to participate in the pastoral care of parishes (can. 517 §2), to preach (can. 766), to serve as the official witness at marriages (can. 1112) and to administer sacramentals (can. 1168).

The above-mentioned roles and functions now open to *women as part of the laity* clearly signal an improvement over their juridic condition in previous legislation. But an accurate perception of the position of women in the new Code cannot be formulated without investigating at least three other key areas. The first consists of those canons that represent a positive alteration of the previous juridic condition of women not merely as *christifideles* but precisely as women. The second consists of those canons which currently place the qualification *viri laici* on members of the *christifideles* thus perpetually excluding women from consideration in regard to their legal content. And the third consists not of canons but of specific application of the law in matters concerning women which potentially leads to different interpretations that impinge directly on the juridic condition of women in practice.

2. WOMEN IN CONTRAST TO MEN

(a) Equalisation of Women

On a very positive note, the 1983 Code has eliminated or altered all but a few of the 1917 Code norms that treated women as functionally subordinate, relatively inept, emotionally unstable or morally suspect. Universal law now recognises the equal status of women with men for determining domicile (can. 104), for changing rite at the time of marriage (can. 112 §1 No.2), for joining associations of the faithful (can. 307 §1) and for choosing the place of ecclesiastical burial (can. 1177). Involvement in financial matters and in administration of ecclesiastical goods of a diocese or other public juridic person as deputed by the competent ordinary is no longer restricted to men (canons 492 §2, 1279 §2). With consistent exceptions made for monasteries of nuns, women and men who are major superiors of religious institutes are equally capable to administer temporal goods (canons 634–640) and to place administrative acts required for transfer, exclaustration and departure of members (canons 684–700). A special assessment of the freedom of women to enter marriage (can. 1067) or consecrated life (canons 641, 656, 658) has been omitted. The new Code has no restriction on the place for hearing confessions of women (can. 964 §3) and has simplified the former elaborate rules regarding confessors for women religious (can. 630). One's sex is no longer named as a factor to be considered in determining the application of penalties (canons 1323–1324). The canons no longer refer directly to the association of clergy with women as potentially suspect (can. 277). Women have ceased to be the last possible legal choice for the minister of baptism (can. 861 §2). And the degrading investigation of the woman in *non-consummatum* marriage cases is now gone (can. 1702).

The 1983 Code does contain a few identifiable differences in the treatment of laywomen and laymen. Except for two instances, however, these retained discrepancies appear to be somewhat reasonable in practice rather than discriminatory in themselves. Among the realistic differences in the treatment of women and men, one norm determines the place of origin for children whose parents have different domicile as the domicile of the mother (can 101 §1) Another establishes a slightly lower minimum age for women to enter marriage validly (can. 1083 §1). Still another limits to women the possibility of being abducted in the marriage impediment of abduction (can. 1089).

In contrast to these, the restriction to men of the stable lay ministries of lector and acolyte (can. 230 §1) is clearly exclusionary. Since it first appeard in *Ministeria quaedam* in 1972, some canonists have referred to this exclusion as inexplicable, curious, discriminatory and sexist. Other canonists accept the exclusion without question because of the traditional connection of these now nominally 'lay' ministries to the reception of sacred orders.[5] Let us describe the exclusion very precisely in its canonical context: the exclusion is contained in a canon within the title 'Obligations and Rights of the Lay Christian Faithful' and limits the ability of a member of the *christifideles laici* to be installed in the ministries of lector and acolyte because of a legal distinction made specifically on the basis of sex.

A second discrepancy constituting a legal distinction made specifically on the basis of sex is the treatment given monasteries of nuns. They alone must observe the extensive and strict norms for papal cloister (can. 667 §3). They alone remain consistently under the vigilance of the diocesan bishop for numerous matters in which other religious—both women and men—are competent to act (canons 615, 625, 637–638, 688). And they alone have instances of Apostolic See intervention directed specifically to them (canons 609 §2, 686 §2). Although the cloistered contemplative life has a long and venerable tradition of special legislation, its selective application to women in the new Code appears as none other than institutional perpetuation of former prejudiced perspectives regarding feminine inferiority.

(b) Women as Excluded from the Clergy

The key distinction among persons in the 1983 Code is not that which identifies women as different from men but, rather, that which distinguishes laity from clergy. Clerics are capable (*habiles*) of possessing and exercising the ecclesiastical power of governance (can. 129 §1). Laity, on the other hand, can only cooperate (*cooperari*) in the exercise of the power of governance and only according to the norm of law (can. 129 §2). Clerics and only clerics can obtain those ecclesiastical offices which require the power of orders or of governance (can. 274 §1). Whereas laity must be judged suitable (*idonei*) before they are capable (*habiles*) of being assumed to offices by the hierarchy (can. 228 §1).[6]

For the *munera* of teaching and sanctifying, members of the laity are also recognised by the new code as having numerous functions and responsibilities. But these are usually highly qualified and carefully circumscribed and are always exercised under the vigilance of, or in subordination to, members of the hierarchy. Thus, the divine institution of *ministri sacri* among the *christifideles* which is expressed as a clergy/lay differentiation in law (can. 207 §1) translates into a very real operational distinction in all aspects of ecclesial life.

Objectively speaking, exclusion from membership in the category of *ministri sacri* constitutes a severe limitation on the use of one's present and potential talent, competence and experience in service of the Church. Similarly, and still objectively speaking, *a priori* categorical exclusion from membership in the category of *ministri sacri* regardless of one's present and potential ability, competence, and experience constitutes a comparable severe loss for the Church. Some men are permanently or temporarily excluded from membership among the *ministri sacri* because they do not possess the qualities (canons 1026–1032), have not fulfilled the requirements (canons 1033–1039), are otherwise impeded by law (canons 1040–1052), or are judged not suitable (can. 1025). All women are perpetually excluded from being considered for possible membership among the *ministri sacri* because they are not men (can. 1024). Suffice it to say that the import of this exclusion for the life of the Church throughout history can only be underestimated. The accuracy of this observation should be evident whether the basis for such exclusion is Augustinian hierarchy, Thomistic anthropology, Scotian divine volition, sacramental signification of the maleness of Jesus, long-standing tradition or, indeed, any combination of these.

(c) Church Law as Applied to Women

Finally, let us recall the earlier comment that law generally flows from and does not dictate the realities of life. This is only partially correct. In a very real sense the legal norms of the Church coupled with the patterns of their consistent application play an integral role in fostering, hindering or retarding the growth of fundamental Christian values, such as the fundamental equality of women and men. Recall also that the content and application of Church law regarding women has had a less than commendable record for its equality over a span of nearly two thousand years.

Thus, it should be no surprise that one can still encounter contemporary interpretations which seem to perpetuate mentalities and attitudes indicative of previous eras. These are clearly evident in the raising of such questions as whether or not a woman is suited to be an episcopal vicar if, indeed, it is even possible for any non-cleric to be one.[7] They are also evident in interpretations that exclude women from functioning as acolytes even though the universal law does not specifically preclude this possibility. Except for the few canons which have been mentioned above, however, the improvement of the juridic condition of women in the 1983 code militates against perpetuating such a mentality and may in the future preclude the raising of such questions.

CONCLUSION

Although the new Church law retains few of the former differences in its treatment of women and men, some of the differences that have been noed are rather significant. This is because: (a) they relate directly or indirectly to the clergy/lay distinction and its correlative exclusion of women from the ranks of *ministri sacri* or (b) they accept without question the subordinate status of women, such as cloistered contemplative women religious, in the Church. In canon 208, the 1983 Code qualifies its affirmation of 'true equality' for all *Christifideles* by adding the phrase 'according to one's own condition and function'. Within this qualification, it can be said that laity are not juridically equivalent to clergy and laywomen are not juridically equivalent to laymen. The former inequality is solidly based on the divine institution of *ministri sacri*; the latter inequality is not so solidly founded.

From a global perspective it is evident that *women are not treated as equal to men in practice either in society or in the Church.* Socially they constitute more than half the world's work force and at least two-thirds of the world's illiterate. They have fewer economic opportunities than men, receive diminished wages in comparison to men and are often politically or physically oppressed by men. Some societies and religions refuse to consider women and men equal, or even potentially equal, in theory. Ecclesially women have traditionally been afforded inferior status in theory and subordinate roles in practice. It cannot be easily or firmly ascertained to what extent the Church has contributed to global and ecclesial inequality through its former legislation and practice. To what extent the new law and practice will contribute to eventual equality of treatment between women and men, both in the Church and in society, still remains to be seen.

Notes

1. McDermott *The Legal Condition of Women in the Church: Shifting Policies and Norms* (Washington, DC. 1979), esp. pp. 1–155. See also D. Morrison *The Juridic Status of Women in Canonical Law and in United States Law* (Rome 1965).

2. J.-M. Aubert *La Femme: antiféminisme et christianisme* (Paris. 1975); K. Børrensen *Subordination et équivalence: Nature et rôle de la femme d'après Augustin et Thomas d'Aquin* (Oslo-Paris 1968);*Sexism and Church Law* ed. J. Coriden (New York 1977); I. Raming *Der Ausschluss der Frau vom priesterlichen Amt: Gottgewollte Tradition oder Diskriminierung?* (Cologne 1973); G. Tavard *Woman in Christian Tradition* (London 1973); E. Schüssler-Fiorenza *In Memory of Her* (New York 1983).

3. The parallel list of comparable 1983 and 1917 code canons concerning laity and women is intended as an aid to the reader but does not claim to be exhaustive and is not identical to similar lists prepared by other canonists. This summary is gleaned from R. McDermott 'Women in the New code' *The Way Supplement* 50 (Summer 1984) 27–37; J. Provost in *The Code of Canon Law: A Text and Commentary* eds. J. Coriden. T. Green, and D. Heintschel (New York 1985) pp. 140–141; F. Urrutia *De normibus generalibus. Adnotationes in codicem: liber I* (Rome 1983) pp. 71–74; M.-T. Van Lunen Chenu and L. Wendholt 'Le Statut de la femme dans le code de droit canonique et dans la convention des Nations Unies' *Praxis juridique et religion* 1 (1984) 7–18.

4. The question of lay persons cooperating in the exercise of the ecclesiastical power of governance and the interplay of canons 129 §2, 145 §2, 228 §1 and 274 §1 have already given rise to conflicting interpretations on the part of contemporary canonists. For an extensive bibliography, a brief explanation of the respective 'German' and 'Roman' schools, and an interpretation demonstrating the potential and/or actual exercise of jurisdiction by laity according to the new code see J. Provost 'Participation of the Laity in the Governance of the Church' *Scudia Canonica* 17 (1983) 417–448. For an interpretation demonstrating the inability of lay persons to hold or exercise jurisdiction according to the same code, see D.-M. Jaeger 'Animadversiones quaedam de necessitudine inter potestatem ordinis et regiminis iuxta C.I.C. recognitum' *Antonianum* 59 (July/December 1984) 628–646. For a scholarly historical analysis of

the documented long-term exercise of jurisdiction by at least some lay persons, and indeed by abbesses, see M. de Fürstenberg 'Exempla iurisdictionis mulierum in Germania septentrionali-orientali' *Periodica* 73 (1984) 89–111.

5. See respectively: F. McManus 'The State of the Liturgy' *Origins* 2 (2 November 1972) 303; J. Allesandro in *Commentary* p. 15; J. Provost *ibid.* p. 141; Van Lunen Chenu and Wentholt, p. 10 *Codigo de derecho canonico*; ed. L. de Echeverria, (Madrid. 1984) pp. 145, 491, 494.

6. Note that, given these legal affirmations, real and/or apparent contradictions appear between offices now open to the laity and the canonical ability of any laity, women or men, to assume and fulfill them. Thus, by canon 1421 §2 a layperson can be constituted in the office of judge, which in itself is an office requiring the power of governance. But, by the same canon, the layperson so constituted can only function as judge when assumed as one lay member of a *collegium* of judges. Likewise, given these legal affirmations, real and/or apparent tensions arise between the new law and current Church practice. Thus, a layperson can hold the office of chancellor which does not require the power of governance (canon 482 §1). But, through use of the canons concerning faculties and delegated power (canons 131–133, 137–144), laypersons who are chancellors can exercise in practice the power of governance for which they are not *habiles* in law. This same lay/cleric distinction regarding governance is also evident in canons concerning consecrated life, such as canons 588 and 596.

7 See A. Gutierrez 'An mulieres possint esse "Vicarii Episcopales"' *Commentarium pro religiosis* 60 (1979) 201–210. Especially p. 210: 'Sed adhuc quaerendum est de capacitate naturali mulieris ad has responsabilitates assumendas . . . .forsan mulieres perquam maxima ex partis minus aptae iudicari possunt ad haec officia sustinenda prout oportet'.

Richard Hill

Religious Life and the Revised Code

INTRODUCTION

RELIGIOUS ARE rapidly becoming accustomed to the revised Code of
Canon Law as it affects their lives and especially as they engage in the
continuing task of revising their constitutions and other internal legislation.
Questions naturally arise, therefore, about difficulties and problems which
they may be encountering in bringing their rules and policies into conformity
with the new universal law and about what the sources of such difficulties may
be. This essay, drawing upon observation and experience, attempts to
compare the new law with the praxis in effect at the time of its promulgation.

It is generally recognised that the canon law for religious, perhaps the most
thoroughly reworked section of the revised Code, *very significantly simplifies
the law it replaces*. A serious effort has been made both to reflect in the new
law the diversity among religious institutes themselves and to respect the
variety of circumstances in which their members live and work. In principle
and in practice it attempts to *balance* the perennially valid elements of the long
tradition of *living according to the evangelical counsels with the need to
introduce greater flexibility in the application of norms common to all
religious communities*. By its numerous references to the constitutions and
other legislation proper to the institutes themselves, the principle of *subsidiary function* is applied with its consequent decentralisation of authority and

decision making with respect to religious congregations. The *homogenisation of religious life*, especially in the case of apostolic institutes, which prevailed over the past century and longer, *is reversed* at least in the universal law.

At the same time the law for religious reflects *its fidelity to the teaching and directives of Vatican II* and its continuity with the post-conciliar interim legislation. This was the charge given to the commission revising the prior Code by Pope John XXIII himself and by his successors. The scores of experts who helped frame the revised law were keenly aware that they were not re-creating religious life, but were providing it with a new juridical framework. Thus, it has come as no surprise that many norms governing religious life were continued in the revised law.

I. LIMITING THE SCOPE

Turning to a comparison between the new legislation and the lived experience, the present reality, of religious life, we are immediately confronted with a major obstacle. The manner in which various religious communities structure and govern themselves and interpret the norms and practices of religious life is so diverse that it defies any certain and specific profile which is universally valid. In some instances there is virtually no comparison among communities. Some have continued without change the model of pre-conciliar religious life, whereas some others appear more similar to secular institutes or associations of the laity. Between these extremes, where most communities are found, there exists a broad spectrum of practice.

What we have to do, therefore, is narrow somewhat the scope of the discussion. To do this we are limiting our assessment to apostolic religious institutes as they are found in the United States and Canada, which are very similar, with some qualifications, to communities in Western Europe. The scope, however, would be too narrow were it limited to institutes whose generalates are located in these two countries or most of whose members reside and work here. While a significant divergence clearly exists between institutes of men and those of women, between large and small congregations and between fully international institutes and those more nationally or regionally identified, such distinctions would not permit a sufficiently general judgment as projected for this paper.

The now well-known Letter of Pope John Paul II to the Bishops of the United States and its appended 'Essential Elements in the Teaching of the Church on Religious Life', although addressed to a single episcopal confer-ence and for a specific purpose, clearly purports to be applicable to all apostolic institutes in the Catholic Church.[1] Despite some puzzling modifications and shifts of emphasis on certain points, it must be admitted that 'Essential Elements' reflects the revised Code of Canon Law and its post-conciliar sources. Among the nine elements or aspects of apostolic religious life which this document identifies we will allude to only four: poverty, obedience-authority, community living and the relationship of institutes and their members to the hierarchy. These four subjects seem to provide an adequate context for comparing the law of the Church with the lived reality of religious communities. Other elements could, of course, be commented upon, but the differences among religious institutes with respect to them would be predictably similar.

2. FOUR ESSENTIAL ELEMENTS

The evangelical counsel of *poverty* as traditionally understood and practiced in religious life implies three things: frugality of life, labour, and dependence of the religious community for all material support (canon 600). The Code says little more than this and remits to the individual institutes to determine more precisely how this frugality, labour and dependence is to be realised. There is great diversity among communities in the application of the general principle. Some institutes leave their members virtually completely free to decide how their income, presuming that they are salaried or otherwise compensated for their work, is disposed of, and require only that a fixed sum of money or a determined percentage of income or a surplus be contributed to the community for the support of members who do not receive salaries or stipends and for the costs of administrations. Most institutes, however, continue to require that any income derived from work or by gift be handed over to the community, which in turn assumes total responsibility for the material support of the members.

The majority of religious institutes provide for a modest degree of independence, through approved budgets, allowances and the like, in the use of money and material possessions and are as generous as they can afford to be in the support of their members. A smaller number of communities continue to expect that permission be obtained for virtually every expenditure, however minor.

The new Code, again reflecting the tradition and the conciliar and post-conciliar teaching, identifies the object of the counsel of *obedience* as submission of will to superiors within the limits established by the constitutions (canon 601). The correlative to this, of course, is the existence of true ecclesial authority in the legitimately named superiors of the institute, a power, the Code asserts, deriving from God through the instrumentality of the Church in the approval of rules and constitutions. While insisting upon the need of councils and broad consultation, the law states that the authority of the superior to make the final decision must be preserved intact (canon 618).

Considering these concepts of obedience and authority out-moded and demeaning for responsible adults, some institutes have abandoned them in favour of what is usually called *personal discernment*. The role of a superior or moderator in this model is limited to participation in the discernment process by way of advice, usually considered an especially important component of the process, but the individual religious makes the final decision for himself or herself and takes responsibility for its consequences. In this construct of authority decisions about oneself are exclusively matters between the individual and his or her conscience enlightened by the discerned will of God. Obedience, therefore, is owed to God, not to a human superior.

In community affairs the superior is restricted to assessing the will of the community itself, to coordinating or moderating the efforts of the individual religious among themselves and to providing for good order. In no event does the superior have the power to make decisions binding upon the group or community. Such binding effect is discovered in the will of the governed and the authority of superiors derives from their acceptance by the members. Similarly, team and collegial governance is widely employed, even in cases where the Code reserves final decisions to individual superiors.

Again it appears that the majority of congregations accept the traditional understanding of the counsel of obedience and acknowledge the personal authority of superiors derived from the constitutions. Through a variety of structures these communities provide extensive consultations proportionate to the importance of the decisions to be made and tend to limit the matters in which an order by a superior is appropriate or necessary. In the day-to-day lives of their members they expect them to make responsible choices and decisions.

In some communities, however, obedience to explicit directives of superiors continues to be understood as necessary in order that even the most ordinary actions may be meritorious and the authority of superiors is exercised with respect to the details of daily life. These institutes, which usually appear to be small and geographically limited, do not seem to provide adequately for consultation and personal initiative.

In the descriptive definition itself of religious institutes the Code preserves the requirement of *life in common* (canon 6507 §2) and the prescription that a community of religious reside in a lawfully designated house under the authority of a superior (canon 608). While most religious institutes insist upon community life wherever possible, it is not uncommon that some will, at least as a matter of policy, permit their members to choose their own living situation. Many religious live alone as a matter of preference or with one or two other members, apart from any need of studies or apostolic work or ministry. At the same time there remain religious houses of excessively large numbers of members which are understandably experienced as oppressive and destructive of a way of life which can truly be called a community.

Finally, the revised Code stresses, as did the Council, that any activity which affects the faithful in general and especially any enterprise or initiative which can be called apostolic or ministerial falls under the *supervision of the bishop* of the diocese where it takes place. The general principle of Vatican II, that the diocesan bishop coordinates and oversees all apostolic works in his diocese, is incorporated as a general norm in canon 394. Thus, in apostolic undertakings or ministries no institute or individual religious is exempt from this supervision and coordination, although there are varying degrees of autonomy depending on what is being done and who is doing it.

While the law presumes that the apostolic work of religious is normally corporate and is subject to the oversight of both the bishop and the community's own superiors and administrators, it allows for individual religious to be named to various ecclesial offices and even to initiate *various projects on their own* with at least the tacit approval of their own superiors and of the bishop or of those who act for him.

Difficulties can arise, however, when individual religious or groups of religious initiate projects or accept secular positions which are called apostolates or even ministries with the backing of their superiors, but which escape the bishop's oversight and coordination with other enterprises of the diocese or which come into conflict with the policies or judgment of the bishop or his administrators.

In order to minimise conflict and to promote cooperation and collaboration the Code, echoing 'Directives for the Mutual Relations Between Bishops and Religious in the Church' of 1978, calls upon bishops and religious to confer with each other, among themselves and with the diocesan clergy. This requires mutually satisfactory organs of consultation and planning (canons 678 3 and 680). This is a responsibility of ecclesial leadership which has only begun to be acknowledged and some structures have been created to carry it out. Thus far they are seldom as effective as they ought to be and run the risk of deteriorating into mere gestures.

In cases where the enterprise undertaken by an individual religious or group of religious is contrary to the wishes or the policies of a bishop and is prohibited by him in his diocese, a few communities, as a matter of policy, consider this purely a conflict situation to be resolved between the individual religious or the group and the diocesan bishop. In such instances the law of the Church and the policy of the institute are clearly at odds with each other.

3. REFLECTION ON PRAXIS

In the four areas above and in others as well some religious communities in Canada and the United States find themselves in *significant conflict with the canon law* as it appears in the 1983 Code. Others—and they seem to be the great majority—have introduced practices which are *in substantial compliance with the law* or can be made so without serious dislocation or dissension. Some communities, however, appear to have made only minimal efforts to take advantage of the freedom which the new law provides them.

In each of these four areas *two clusters of values contend* for the ascendency. In the arenas of poverty, authority, obedience, community living and apostolate, *individual freedom, fulfillment, worth and autonomy* contend with the inevitable constraints or limitations of *tradition and law*. When such personal goods are so highly valued that they preclude practically any limitations, these dimensions of religious life can be so relativised that their meaning and its implications become purely a matter of personal definition and choice.

In other cases, however, in which the goods of tradition and law are so valued that personal choice and freedom is practically meaningless and is confined to narrowly circumscribed boundaries, personal initiative and responsibility can be sacrificed for the sake of uniformity and conformity. This can pose a serious threat to the spiritual and psychological health of the human person and only the immature and insecure will be attracted. Neither extreme is viable.

The great majority of religious communities and individual religious have discovered a balance between law and respect for personal freedom and integrity. A poverty of ultimately total dependence upon and accountability to a religious community for material support has been successfully designed by most religious institutes without stripping the individual of responsibility and choice. They have also created an authority-obedience balance which is liberating and productive without compromising the authority of superiors or the good of willing obedience. Styles of community living, which are supportive of individuals and respectful of their legitimate privacy seem to abound among North American religious without deteriorating into boarding houses or exclusive clubs. Finally, the great majority of religious institutes and individual religious are finding it relatively easy to relate cooperatively and constructively with the dioceses and their departments and parishes without privatising ministry in the Church or anointing every kind of activity as ministry.

CONCLUSION

Assuming, then, that this assessment of the lived reality of contemporary religious life in North America, however general and imprecise, is accurate, we come to the question posed for this essay. Is the revised law for religious in harmony with the living reality? It is my contention that, with the evident exception of the most radical extremes, the law is presently adequate and workable. It can be reasonably understood and implemented as liberating persons for service, as securing their rights and promoting a sense of community and fellowship. It is also my perception, however, that the law is being misread and misinterpreted at several important points, mostly in an excessively restrictive sense, and the resulting misunderstanding is unnecessarily causing disquiet and alienation in some communities. When, on the other hand, the nature and values of religious life enunciated by Vatican II and reiterated and further developed by such documents as *Renovationis causam, Evangelica testificatio,* and *Mutae relationes*[2] are not considered relevant, much less normative, for religious, then the revised Code as it relates to religious institutes will also be judged as essentially defective.

What is needed at this point in time is a correct understanding of the revised Code and of the broad flexibility and adaptability incorporated in it. At the same time it is equally necessary to monitor and discuss the ongoing applicability of specific norms as we gain experience with the new Code. In the future it is inevitably going to be necessary to propose amendments of the law because the needs of the Church and of its religious institutes will certainly change.

Notes

1. The text of John Paul II's letter to the Bishops of the United States, and of the document 'Essentials Elements' which accompanied it, have not been published in the *AAS.* They did appear in *Origins* 13/8 (7 July 1983) 129, 131–142. For an indepth study see *Religious Life in the U.S. Church: The New Dialogue* ed. Robert J. Daly et al. (New York 1984).

2. See Congregation for Religious and Secular Institutes, instruction *Renovationis causam* 6 January 1969: *AAS* 61 (1969) 103–120; Paul VI, apostolic exhortation *Evangelica testificatio* 29 June 1971: *AAS* 63 (1971) 497–526; Congregation for Bishops and Congregation for Religious and Secular Institutes directives *Mutuae relationes* 14 May 1978: *AAS* 70 (1978) 473–506.

PART III

Reception

John Faris

One View from Eastern Catholic Churches on the New Latin Code of Canon Law

ALTHOUGH THE 1983 Revised *Codex Iuris Canonici* (RCIC) opens with an absolute assertion *restricting the extent of its concern to the Latin Church* (can. 1), an examination of the provisions of this Code reveals that it also does indeed have *resonances in the Eastern Catholic churches*. This, all Catholics of both East and West are called upon to accommodate themselves to this new Code of the Latin Church.

Provisions treating the relations between Catholic churches are commonly designated as 'interritual'. However, a more accurate term is 'interecclesial', since the subject is precisely the canonical relationship between ecclesial communions within the Catholic Church.

That such interecclesial provisions are to be found in the Latin Code is to be expected. During Vatican I[1] and Vatican II[2] proposals were made that there should be a single common code for all the Catholic churches of both East and West. This code would include the *ius commune* of all the Catholic churches while other specific matters would be left to the *ius proprium* of the respective churches. Such a code was never deemed suitable for a variety of reasons. Therefore, the codes of the Latin and Eastern churches are for us the only possible *fora* for such provisions.

The need for these provisions is acutely felt today for a variety of reasons. The past century has witnessed a massive immigration of Eastern Catholic faithful to the Western hemisphere. The resulting phenomenon is that Latin and Eastern Catholics are living in a symbiotic relationship. The frequent interaction of Catholic faithful from the West and East requires appropriate norms governing their relations. Further, as a result of the impetus given at the Second Vatican Council[3] the hierarchies of many Eastern Catholic churches have been established in the Western hemisphere.[4] Due to the multiplicity of hierarchies in a given area, questions of jurisdiction, canonical status of the faithful, and sacramental life have arisen.

The juridical relationship between the Latin and Eastern Catholic churches is a delicate matter in so far as not a few difficulties and misunderstandings have arisen in the past. Therefore, before addressing those specific instances wherein the Latin Code provides norms governing the relationship between the Catholic churches of East and West, it is useful to treat a few ecclesiological and canonical notions which will influence our perception of these norms.

1. A COMMUNION OF CATHOLIC CHURCHES

It is common for Western ecclesiology and canonistics to identify the Catholic Church with the Latin Church. The Eastern Catholic churches are consequently misconstrued as abnormal administrative divisions or ecclesial appendage to this Latin/Catholic Church. Such an ecclesial model is not only erroneous and offensive to Eastern Catholics, but it also does not conform to reality. The Catholic Church cannot be identified with any individual church or rite. Rather, the Church is a communion of Catholic churches (*communio ecclesiarum Catholicarum*) of both East and West. Each of these Catholic churches, while united in the same faith, sacraments and government, constitute separate moral persons and follow their own specific form of a rite.[5] This diversity of legitimate traditions should not be perceived as injurious to Catholic unity. Instead, such a diversity serves to emphasise the ability of the Church to integrate a variety of manifestations of the Christian faith into one communion.

With reference to the legal stature of these churches, canon law describes them as *sui iuris*, i.e., capable of self-governance in all matters excepting those reserved to the Roman Pontiff or ecumenical councils.[6] All of the ritual churches *sui iuris* (to use the terminology of the RCIC)[7] are equal in consideration of rank, rights and obligations.[8]

A schematic model of the Church would place the ritual church *sui iuris* in an intermediate position between the universal Church and the diocese. Such a *tripartite ecclesial model* has been discussed in recent years, but is not yet common.[9] Western ecclesiology usually portrays the church as two-tiered: on the one tier, there is the universal church which is governed by the Roman Pontiff; on the second tier are the dioceses, each of which is governed by an individual bishop. Consequently, the ritual churches *sui iuris*, in their intermediate position position, are conceived as something extraneous to the essential constitution of the Church.

Yet it is the ritual church *sui iuris* which allows for the Church, as the Body of Christ, to be catholic, i.e., capable of sustaining *a legitimate diversity in culture, spirituality, theology, liturgy and discipline.* The diocese is too small an ecclesial entity to provide the required support for such variety. The universal Church is too vast to address such particular matters. Only the ritual church *sui iuris*, as an ecclesial entity usually comprised of several dioceses, can perform such a function.

There are many ramifications to the adoption of this tripartite ecclesial model. The intermediate level of ecclesial communion provides the necessary framework for future unity among the Christian churches. The divided churches and communions of both East and West can enter into full Catholic communion without forsaking their unique ecclesial identities which have developed during the past centuries. Churches which are still outside the Catholic Church (e.g., Anglican) could enter into the fullness of Catholic communion as a ritual church *sui iuris* and follow their own rites.

This tripartite ecclesial model will also provide for possible ecclesial development within the Latin Church itself. At the present time there are a variety of communities with different cultural backgrounds but which all follow the Latin rite. Voices have been raised which call for the right of these communities to develop in terms of their unique expressions of culture, theology, liturgy, and canonical discipline, i.e., rite. Thus, in France, the Philippines or Ghana, there exists the possibility of ritual churches *sui iuris* developing out of the Latin Church.

Let us now proceed with an examination of those instances in the Latin Code wherein the life of the Eastern Catholic churches will be affected. The limitations of space do not permit me to provide details of all the various facets of interecclesial relations.[10] Therefore, only those areas which are of general interest will cursorily be addressed.

2. THE LATIN CODE AND EASTERN CATHOLIC CHURCHES

(a) Membership in a Ritual Church sui iuris.

Faithful are never members of the Catholic Church 'at large'. One is always a member of a specific ritual church *sui iuris* such as the Ukrainian Church, the Latin Church, the Armenian Church, or the Maronite Church. Membership in a ritual Church is a crucial factor in the life of a Catholic: it determines an individual's public and personal prayer life (liturgy and spirituality), Christian lifestyle (discipline), his expression of Christian revelation (theology), and the dynamics of a social group (culture and jurisdiction). Therefore, the abandonment or adoption of a ritual Church is much more significant than the transfer from one diocese to another within the same ritual Church. Like its predecessor, the 1917 Code, the RCIC includes provisions governing the acquisition of membership in a ritual Church and the transfer of membership from one ritual church to another.

There has been a significant change in the discipline of the RCIC when compared with the 1917 Code. In the 1917 Code, the ritual church of the father (or the mother if the father was a non-Catholic) was the criterion which determined the ritual church of baptism for the child. The RCIC stipulates that it is the *choice of the parents* (if they are members of different Catholic churches) that determines the ritual church of either parent as the church of baptism for the child. The ritual church of the father is determinant only when this agreement is lacking. Since there are some situations wherein the decision of the parents will be difficult to ascertain, the determination of a person's membership in a ritual church will be a more difficult task for canonists in the future.

A non-baptised person who is at least fourteen years old is free to choose the ritual Church in which he or she desires to be baptised (can. 111 §2). The RCIC is silent concerning the membership of a baptised non-Catholic who enters into Catholic communion. However, the Second Vatican Council stipulates that a baptised person is obliged to enter the Catholic counterpart of his former non-Catholic Church.[11] There is some question as to whether this obligation is for the sake of validity or lawfulness.

Confirmation administered by an Eastern priest (Catholic or non-Catholic) to the faithful of any ritual church (including the Latin) is always valid.[12] Latin bishops and priests who have the proper faculties also administer the sacrament validly to all the faithful (can. 882). For lawfulness the particular law of each ritual church *sui iuris* must be consulted. In danger of death any priest can confirm validly and lawfully (can. 883 §3).

An individual is free to receive the sacrament of the Eucharist (can. 923). penance (can. 991), and anointing of the sick (can. 1003 §2) from a priest of any Catholic church. However, the reception of sacraments in a ritual church other than one's own, for whatever length of time, does not constitute a transfer of membership (can. 112 §2).

It has been the practice of the Catholic Church to encourage the faithful to maintain membership in their respective ritual Churches even if they emigrate from the place of origin of the ritual church. Although the Church has at various times modified the factors which determine the acquisition or transfer of membership in a ritual church, the transfer of domicile has not been crucial.

There are, however, occasions wherein persons desire to transfer from one Catholic church to another. The RCIC provides for such transfers. Upon entering a marriage or during its course, a spouse (not just the wife as was the case in the 1917 Code) can transfer to the ritual church of the other spouse. Upon dissolution of the marriage, the spouse is free to return to the Latin Church (can. 112 §1, 2°). An unmarried person can also transfer to another ritual church in virtue of permission granted by the Apostolic See (can. 112 §1, 1°).

(b) Interecclesial Marriage Law

A Latin priest (ordinary, pastor or a delegated priest/deacon) validly assists at a marriage within the confines of his territory provided at least one of the parties is a member of the Latin Church (can. 1109). The RCIC is silent about interecclesial marriages involving a Latin and an Eastern Catholic. According to the provisions of the 1917 CIC (can. 1097 §2) and Eastern canon law (*Crebrae Allatae*, can. 88 §3), such a marriage was to be celebrated according to the rite and before the pastor of the groom for the sake of lawfulness. The silence on the part of the RCIC concerning this matter indicates that this stipulation is no longer in force in cases involving a Latin and an Eastern Catholic. (In cases involving two Eastern Catholics from different ritual churches, the provisions of *Crebrae Allatae*, can. 88 §3 are still to be applied.)

There are differences in the impediments stipulated by the RCIC and the *ius vigens* of the Eastern Catholic churches in the areas of consanguinity, affinity, public propriety, adoption, guardianship, and spiritual relationship. Although such cases are quite rare, pastors should be aware of the disparity of disciplines.

(c) Bishops Conferences

RCIC canon 450 §1 provides that the Eastern Catholic bishops can be invited to join the local bishops' conference, in which case they enjoy only a consultative vote unless the statutes of the conference stipulate otherwise. Such a provision is more restrictive than the prior legislation of *Christus Dominus*, n. 38, (2) which included the Eastern bishops in the bishops' conferences and placed no restruction on their right to vote.

The exclusion of Eastern bishops from the bishops' conferences can have a variety of negative consequences. Of major concern is the weakening of the 'Catholic voice' in a given country or region. Quite often there are issues or areas of common interest which should be addressed by a united Catholic community. The exclusion of a group of Eastern Catholic bishops (whose numbers are sometimes significant) would naturally weaken the ability of a conference to speak and act effectively.

Another consequence of the exclusion of Eastern bishops from the bishops' conferences would be the creation of two bishops' conferences: one Eastern and one Latin. In certain areas, there is quite a bit of misunderstanding between the Latin and Eastern Catholic churches. The bishops' conferences, composed of bishops from all the Catholic churches in a given area, can provide a forum for open discussion and eventual cooperation.

(d) Patriarchs

An Eastern patriarch can become a member of the College of Cardinals (retaining as his title his patriarchal see) and therefore participate in the decision-making process (e.g., papal elections) at the highest level of the Church (can. 350 §3). It is beneficial to have representatives from all Catholic churches participating in the election of the Successor of Peter. An alternative arrangement would have been to grant the patriarchs the right to vote in certain matters. Such a right would be distinct from membership in the College of Cardinals.

3. THE FUTURE CODE FOR THE EASTERN CATHOLIC CHURCHES

A discussion of the canonical renewal in the Latin Church would be incomplete without mention of e project of codification and revision that is presently taking place in the Easte Catholic churches.

During this interim period before the promulgation of the Eastern Catholic Code, certain stipulations of the RCIC have created a certain imbalance between the Latin and Eastern churches. For example, according to the provisions of RCIC canon 111 §1, an Eastern Catholic father and a Latin mother can choose to have their child baptised in the Latin Church. However, a strict interpretation of the canon will not permit a Latin father and Eastern Catholic mother to baptise their child in the Eastern Catholic church. Another example is RCIC canon 112 §1, 2°, which allows for a Latin husband to transfer to the Eastern Catholic church of his wife. However, neither this canon nor Eastern canon law (*Cleri Sanctitati*, can. 8) allows an Eastern Catholic husband to transfer to the Latin Church of his wife. It is hoped that the future Eastern Code will clarify the ambiguities and rectify the imbalances that currently exist. Just as the Eastern Catholic churches have been obliged to accommodate themselves to the provisions of the 1983 Latin Code, so too will the Latin Church be called upon to adapt itself to the future Eastern Code.

Notes

1. J.D. Mansi *Sacrorum Conciliorum Nova et Amplissima Collectio* (Graz p161) 49: 1087–88.

2. *Acta Synodalia Sacrosancti Concilii Oecumenici Vaticani II*, II, Pat V, p. 36.

3. *Orientalium Ecclesiarum* n. 4.

4. According to the provisions of canon law, parts of Europe, North and South America and Australia are properly designated as 'Eastern territories'. See *Postquam Apostolicis* canon 303 §1, 3.

5. See *Orientalium Ecclesiarum*, n. 2; *Lumen gentium* nn. 13d and 23d.

6. *Postquam Apostolicis* canon 303 §1, 1°.

7. See, for example, canons 111 and 112. Many objections have been raised to the use of the term 'ritual church *sui iuris*'. It ramains to be seen if the future Eastern Code will employ this term or 'particular church' for the designation of these ecclesial communions.

8. See S.C. Prop. Fide, 15 June, 1867, *Codificazione Canonica Orientale*, Fonti, Fasciocolo II, p. 449 and *Orientalium Ecclesiarum* nn. 3 & 8.

9. George Nedungatt 'Autonomy, Autocephaly, and the Problem of Jurisdiction Today' *Kanon* 5 (1981) 19–35.

10. Together with Victor J. Pospishil, I have treated these matters in some detail in a booklet entitled *The New Latin Code of Canon Law and Eastern Catholics* (Brooklyn, NY 11209).

11. *Orientalium Ecclesiarum* n. 4.

12. *Orientalium Ecclesiarum* n. 14, does not make a distinction between a Catholic and a non-Catholic priest, stating only that 'All priests of an Eastern rite can confer this sacrament validly . . .'

Albert Stein

The New Codex: Its Echo in the Churches of the German Reformation

THE APPEARANCE of a new law book for the Roman Catholic Church may be expected to call forth an echo, among non-Catholic churches, primarily from those churches whose membership is numerically roughly similar, i.e., where the two churches have a neighbourly interest in one another. Experts consider that there will be no echo only where the non-Catholic neighbour churches also have a canon law which is the subject of systematic study. Both these situations can be found today in the German-speaking world. This brief exposition will therefore restrict itself to publications originating in that linguistic area.

It must be said that, so far, very little has appeared in Protestant German language journals on this topic. I have not been able to evaluate more than eight more or less presentable responses in what follows[1-8]. I can only hazard a guess as to why this is so. It is well known that canon law is not a high priority in the Protestant churches. Martin Luther's reformation was originally sparked off by Catholic canon law; thus it may not be the most inviting aspect of Catholicism to prospective Protestant readers. The fact that the new *Codex Iuris Canonici* was initially published only in Latin may have made it more difficult to arrive at a scholarly evaluation. All the same, Protestant publications in the last few years have contained more about Catholic canon law than for decades. Yet the echo has been faint up to now, and not without contradictions. What follows is a brief synopsis, arranged under various heads.

On the positive side, there is a welcome for the fact that the new canon law book for the Catholic Church has been produced at all. An expert critic such as the President of the Canon Law Institute of the Evangelical Church in Germany calls the new Codex 'a great achievement of modern legislation'.[1] This view is all the more understandable since, a few years ago, regrettably and after long planning, an attempt to reform the constitution of the Evangelical Church in Germany came to nothing. Several critics emphasise the fact that the new canon law is not only constructed differently and more theologically than its predecessor, but also that it is shorter and more clearly arranged.[1,8] There is criticism, however, both as regards the secret procedures, particularly in the final phase of the preparation of law,[6] and of the flaws in the production of the first impression;[8] the particular flavour of the semi-official German translation is also queried.[8]

Writers are glad to stress that the new canon law, in accord with the Council's wishes, has a more definitely ecumenical orientation; but it is felt that this intention is not carried out equally in all areas; not all the hopes which had been raised have been fulfilled.[1,5,6,8] One commentator sees a commendable desire to avoid a narrow formalism in the fact that the introductory constitution speaks of the primacy of love, grace and the charisms within an ecclesial order, emphasising that the goal of the enterprise is to facilitate an orderly progress in the life of the Church and of the men and women who belong to it. It is noted that the new Codex ends, in canon 1752, with the words: the highest law must be what ministers to the salvation of souls.[8]

Quite naturally, Protestant reviewers examine these high principles of the new Codex with a view primarily to the traditional controversies and the problems involved in churches living side by side. It is noted with regret that, in the area of constitutional law, the pope (in can. 331) is referred to as Vicar of Christ; at this point the new canon law lags behind the Council and manifests—as elsewhere—traces of a conflict between conciliar, episcopalist ideas and papal tendencies towards 'restauration'.[6] The result is that the papacy is strengthened by the new Codex; in spite of the principle of subsidiarity, the Church is governed more from above downwards;[3] regional leadership is attenuated.[2] By contrast, however, other reviewers expect the future to bring positive development, precisely through the implementation of the new conditions concerning the full exercise of power by the bishops and bishops' conference.[1,8]

Canon law's discovery of the 'non-ordained Christian' is heralded as a substantial improvement in the law of the person; unfortunately, the rights of the person are formulated very cautiously, and compared with the teaching of the Council there is a detectable tendency to dilute them.[1] In this same issue, however, other writers see a visible attempt to create room for action and to facilitate adaptations.[4,6] Yet even in the new form, the Reformation's concern for the priesthood of all believers still seems not to have been recognised,[5] nor have doubts about its basis been dissolved.[2]

The case is similar with the law concerning sacraments. In the field of baptismal doctrine, the separated churches largely share the same theological basis. But in the area of law, regrettably, grievances arise. To say, with canon 868 §2 that a child may be baptised even against the wishes of its non-Catholic parents, is to stand the ecumenical insight on its head.[4] One critic regrets with much pain that evangelical Christians are still not accepted as godparents,[1] while another discerns progress in the fact that they can be recognised as witnesses to the baptism.[4] Protestant critics[7] naturally protest at the disciplinary procedure of canon 1366 (which is also disputed by certain Catholic authors) regarding parents who do not present their children for Catholic baptism;[7] all that one can hope for here is that the norms will be applied sensitively.[4]

The new rules for shared worship between Catholics and Protestants arouse painful emotions. The only positive feature is that now 'even' non-Catholics may be given blessings and, where need arises, a church burial.[4] Developments in the area of intercommunion, however, seem to be practically 'frozen'.[6] Still, one of the critics regards the law's silence on the question of 'ecumenical worship' and on what is meant by the 'serious necessity' in canon 844 §4, which would allow administering the sacrament to non-Catholics, as an opportunity for the bishops' conferences to lay down favourable conditions.[3] Ultimately there is a recognition that the rest of all legal problems is the failure, so far, to reach theological agreement on the question of ministry.[1]

As is well known, the fact that there cannot be full shared worship is a particularly grievous problem for marriages and families where the spouses belong to, and endeavour to remain faithful to, different Christian churches. They are given little help by the provisions of the new canon law on what are, regrettably, still called 'mixed marriages' in the heading of canon 1124. While the change from the system of dispensations to that of licences in the law on mixed marriages is acknowledged to be an emphasis on the distinct nature of this area, over against that of the other classical impediments to marriage, the criticism is that the new Codex has drawn no seminal conclusions from this realisation, and thus, for all practical purposes, has maintained the legal status quo ante.[4] It is welcomed as a sign of progress that, contrary to the general principle of canon,[11] a person who formally leaves the Catholic Church is no longer subject to the norms concerning the canonical form of marriage (can. 1124);[1] hope is no longer entertained for a general dispensation for all mixed marriages on German territory.[4,7] It is felt that the opportunity of Protestants to appear on the 'shiny parquet floor' of Catholic marriage tribunals will prove to be problematical.[4] Thus the new canon law situation is not seen to provide a permanent solution.[6]

No doubt there will be further and more nuanced Protestant assessments of the new Roman canon law, once its provisions, which are drawn up for the whole world, have been concretely applied to the local situation by diocesan regulations and have taken effect. Until then the Protestant attitude will perhaps be best illustrated by the observation of an evangelical author[9] which has since been cited with approval by a Catholic expert:[10]

'In general it must be said that the new canon law does not make dialogue between Christians any easier, nor does it render it significantly harder; what it does is to provide a clear basis for it. To the extent that evangelical Christians have been disappointed in their hopes of tangible progress, such hopes were evidently premature. In its broad principles the new Code surely does present new possibilities for an ecumenical rapprochement of separated Christians. Bishops' conferences, bishops and tribunal judges, as well as all others who are involved in applying the new law, will have opportunities of clearly implementing the Code's ecumenical options even in the application of difficult individual regulations, until such time as a further drawing-together of separated Christians presses us to revise the canon law further with a view to expressing a more juridically perfected as well as a greater unity.'

Translated by Graham Harrison

Notes

1. Axel Frh. v. Campenhausen 'Der Codex Iuris Canonici, evangelische Bemerkungen' in *MD, Materialdienst des Konfessionskundl. Instituts* (Bensheim) 1/85, 3–6.

2. Hans Dombois *Das Recht der Gnade, Ökumenisches Kirchenrecht III* (Bielfeld 1983) 356f., 364f., 391.

3. Reinhard Frieling 'Rechtsform im Vatikan' in *Evangelische Kommentare* 16 (Stuttgart 1983) 128–130.

4. Heiner Grote 'Zum neuen Gesetzbuch der kath. Kirche, Überlegungen aus evangelische-ökumenischer Sicht' in *Beiträge zum Kirchenrecht, Akademievorträge 16* ed. Gerhard Krems (Schwerte 1984) pp. 8–24.

5. Hans Martin Müller 'Lutherisches Kirchenverständnis und der Begriff des

Codex Iuris Canonici 1983' in *Zeitschrift für evangelisches Kirchenrecht 29* (Tübingen 1984) 546–559.

6. Peder Nørgaard-Højen 'Das Papstamt bleibt bestimmend, zur Revision des katholischen Kirchenrechts' in *Lutherische Monatshefte 24* (Hamburg 1985) 129–154.

7. Walter Schöpfsdau *Konfessionsverschiedene Ehen, ein Handbuch. Bensheimer Hefte 61* (Göttingen 1984) 52–58.

8. Albert Stein 'Der neue Codex des kanonischen Rechtes Papst Johannes Paul II. und das einführende römische-katholische Schrifttum' in *Theologische Literaturzeitung 109* (Leipzig 1984) 787–795.

9. Albert Stein 'Die Bedeutung des neuen Codex fur die Ökumene' in *Actio Catholica*, fasc. 2 (Vienna 1983) 16.

10. Heribert Heinemann 'Ökumenische Implikationen des neuen kirchlichen Gesetzbuches' in *Catholica 39* (Münster 1985) 26.

Steven Bwana

The Impact of the New Code in Africa

INTRODUCTION

WHEN POPE John XXIII called for the reform of the 1917 Code of Canon Law, the move was seen by many as long overdue. Together with the call for the Second Vatican Council, many Catholics at large, and canonists and theologians in particular, believed that at last the Roman Catholic leadership was rediscovering itself and adapting to the changes at the times.

It was of particular interest to many Africans because these changes were being debated in the Church at the same time when most of their countries obtained *political independence*. To conservative Christians all these changes could not be understood easily. For progressives, they symbolised hope.

Twenty-five years later the new Code of Canon Law has come into force. The theological changes introduced under the controversial papacy of Paul VI are well rooted now even though there are already calls for their review!

To an African theologian or canonist some basic questions still linger. Do these so-called changes reflect or accommodate African reality? Or better still, *are our particular churches really African?*

I. THE AFRICAN SITUATION

As Pope John Paul II himself stated in his apostolic constitution promulgating it, the new code aims to make the *laws be truly in accord with the salvific mission of the Church*. Upon examination, the new Code is more pastoral than the 1917 one. As Pope Benedict XV implied in his *motu proprio* of 15 September, 1917, the former Code stressed juridical reorganisation, centralisation and systematisation of Church power in the hands of the Roman Pontiff, a departure from the traditional approach even since the Council of Trent.

The 1983 Code reflects the changes initiated by the Second Vatican Council. It gives the legal touch to those changes.

There is no evidence that sub-Sahara Africa was represented at the Council of Trent, let alone that its values were realised by the then known world. At Vatican II that part of Africa was fairly represented physically, even though most of those representatives had been 'mented' in Rome or Europe. Those Africans on the preparatory Commission for the Code were no different. Therefore, what is the impact of the Code for Africa?

Indeed one does not have to restrict the above question to the Code alone. All forms of laws that were imported had far reaching consequences for the African reality. The Continental system brought by the French and Portugese proved alien to Africans. The Anglo-Saxon tradition was and remains too complex to be admired by the majority of the people as promoting justice.

Hand-in-hand, there is a well-observed (even though in many societies unwritten) African traditional system of settling disputes, of worshipping, etc. It is no surprise, therefore, that an *African theology is evolving*. The next step, I believe, will be the *evolution of an African Canon Law* emanating from this theology.

All the alien laws, including the Code, have never been at 'peace' with the African situation in most cases. The end result of this situation is the continued coexistence of an African who is a Christian on Sunday and holydays, but a traditionalist during the other days. It may be argued that such situations are temporary, and that given the rapid changes (political, economic, social, etc.) Africa is undergoing, they will vanish. In most countries the Christian Church is hardly 150 years old. To entertain the above argument we would have to look ahead 150 years; it is therefore not easy to come to a reasonable conclusion.

2. THE IMPACT IN AFRICA

Although pastorally oriented the Code has not lost its other basic character, that of being an organ of the Church that gives and guarantees the normative authority of the Roman Pontiff over the entire Church. Part II, section I of

Book II shows this. The reason usually advanced is that the centralised authority of the pope guarantees unity and uniformity for the universal Church (can. 333). However, if the salvific mission entrusted to the Church is to be realised, then the *diocesan bishops need to play a more prominent role* than the one provided for in Chapter II of Section II of Book II.

This necessity arises from the truth that bishops are the ones who face the day-to-day realities within which the people of God live. Failure to have them play a more important role in the Church invites the danger of having an exteriorly united Church which is failing in its salvific mission interiorly. If this necessity cannot be granted to individual particular churches, then the role of the episcopal conferences (another positive element in the new code) should be strengthened by giving them more authority than the rubber stamp they seem to be in the current law (canons 447-459).

3. MARRIAGE

There is nothing in the Code which is more touchy for most Christians in Africa than marriage. The new Code (Book IV, Part I, Title VII) contains a lot of analytical improvement. However, there is no substantive departure from the former Code, notwithstanding the aspect of pastoral care (canons 1063-1072). That being the case, some of the *basic differences that existed between the former code and the reality in Africa remain unresolved.* Some of these basic differences are analysed below.

(a) Definition

While the 1917 Code developed gradually in successive canons (canons 1012, 1013, and 1081) what marriage is, the new Code (can. 1055) shows clearly what marriage is—*a covenant between a man and a woman.* As such it entails consent, and rights and obligations of the parties to each other. When it is between Christians it is elevated to the dignity of a sacrament, hence beyond human power to dissolve it. This definition itself is a subject of discussion in many aspects.

Modern Africans are rapidly changing in favour of the principle of consent between the parties. It is important for the two—a man and a woman—to have the final say in the marriage they want to enter; but this is contrary to the tradition up to now, which is still very strong among some rural tribes, by which the parents or guardians of both parties have the final say.

However, the African need for parental consent was (and still is) not that bad. It meant something in relation to marriage, which was seen principally as an alliance between two clans and only secondarily as a union between the individuals. From that understanding the two clans became jointly responsible for the success (or termination in case there was an irreparable breakdown) of that marriage and the new family at large. Obviously this kind of relationship meant, and still means, that marriage is oriented to the lineal family. Hence it is considered a *communal and social affair as opposed to the mere contractual relationship between the two*—the kind of relationship which is reflected in the Code. This positive aspect of African life ought to have been reflected in the Code; or, as canons 12 and 13 tend to show, the particular churches in Africa ought to incorporate this fundamental principle in their particular laws.

(b) Impediments

Most of the impediments in the Code are also acceptable in the African way of life. The basic difference is with sterility. Canon 1084 §3 states that sterility does not invalidate a marriage unless, of course, it is interpreted together with canon 1098. Does this cater to the fears of family-conscious Christians such as Africans? I believe so.

In many nullity cases which have come to Church tribunals in recent years in Tanzania, sterility seems to be the source of the claims; both canons 1084 and 1098 have been interpreted jointly in favour of a party (usually the man) who alleges to have been deceived.

Sterility is a big problem because to an African, marriage is an alliance between clans and has to continue the stream of communal life through the begetting of children. Failure to do so amounts to blocking that stream, hence blocking the work of procreation. It is not strange, therefore, that this tradition goes hand-in-hand with the one that considers *marriage consummated only after the birth of a child to that marriage*.

(c) Celebration

The form of celebration of marriage is not a problem to Africans once all the prerequisites have been complied with. Whether the parties really follow or believe in the Church ceremony is a question beyond the ambit of this paper. What is important and worth mentioning here is that to date, the celebrations in the canonical ceremony are *preceded or succeeded by another ceremony which observes the traditional rites*, the provisions of canon 1127, §3 notwithstanding. There are theological and canonical reasons for this behaviour, including what was already stated earlier: to be a Christian on

Sunday and holydays, but a traditionalist the rest of the time. Christianity has yet to be lived by the ordinary African in his environment.

(d) Effects

The canons on the effect of marriage (canons 1134–1140) contain many positive elements, yet these are themselves sources of continuing conflict in African societies. The three basic elements mentioned here are: (i) the permanent and exclusive nature of marriage; (ii) equality between the parties; (iii) children.

(i). The permanent and exclusive nature of marriage by itself is a *challenge to polygamy*, whether simultaneous or successive. Described as one of the oldest patterns of African marriage life, polygamy as an institution contributes more to a modern trend of marriage instability. It is a 'plague' whose growth in many tribes was historically related to social, economic and psychological problems.

Economically, polygamy guaranteed the supply of human labour which was the major source of the work force. The introduction of automation contributed strongly against the continued vitality of polygamy. Socially, polygamy guaranteed the privileged and exploitative position of a husband who was the head of a family with extensive powers but few responsibilities. Modern developments which make African women increasingly aware of their role have contributed to the fight against polygamy. Psychologically, the more wives a man had the more prestigiously he was regarded. He could have more children to enrich him (girls, through dowry) or to defend him (boys, in cases of conflicts, wars, etc.). With the continued stability and reduced inter-tribal wars, these reasons are no longer important.

Christianity, and particularly Roman Catholicism, added the final nail to the coffin by preaching in favour of monogamy.

(ii). There cannot be equality between parties if polygamy flourishes. However, with all its positive elements, equality between parties still has a long way to go to root itself in Africa. It is challenged by other factors, such as the poor position in which African women find themselves. Educationally they are still less fortunate in many countries than men. Economically, they are also less fortunate even though they are the ones who do most of the productive work. However, the stress on equality in the Code obviously is more than merely educational or financial. In family life there ought to be an understanding that both parties are one and have the same rights and privileges, centred on true Christian love as taught by the Church.

(iii). The code emphasises more of a *nuclear type of marriage* in contrast to the African concept, which is *more communitarian*. When it comes to the question of children the emphasis is the same. Under the Code, parents seem to have all the responsibility. In traditional life the parents have responsibility, but the clan shares it. Even though canon 1136 does not encompass this idea, that fact that it states (and correctly) that parents have the *most* (emphasis mine) grave obligation implies that there are others who share that responsibility as well. Contemporary African canonists tend to support the application of both principles. In cases of marital breakdown, children brought up in a communitarian way face less misery than those under the nuclear family system.

(e) Dissolution

Remarkably not altered in the Code is the indissolubility of marriages in the Catholic Church generally, and especially those between two baptised persons if consummation has taken place. The few exceptions (the Pauline and Petrine privileges) have not been altered much.

Faced by many problems of marriage breakdown in recent years, the Church in many countries—Tanzania included—has found itself faced with increasing claims of nullity. The tendency seems to be leaning towards a wider interpretation of procedural law, reflecting indirectly on the strong cultures held by the people but which do not expressly contravene the provisions of the Code. Such precedents, however, do not go far enough, and sometimes are revised by higher tribunals in the Church. One may therefore conclude that in regard to nullity procedures, the new Code has not gone far as well.

4. WHAT NEXT?

Marriage is but one of many matters covered by the Code which, even though there is improvement, still leave much to be desired. Equally important not only to Africa but throughout the world is the question of the *role and place of the laity in the Church.* They make up well over ninety per cent of all the faithful, but their role is insignificantly codified.

Women are also not fairly recognised. Theological and biblican citations are usually advanced by the male dominated hierarchy to support the *status quo.* There are other important matters where the Code is seen in many parts of the world either as lacking comprehensive treatment, or simply as maintaining the *status quo.* All the above lead to a view held for some time that many laws only depict the *status quo.* They do not march with the ongoing changes in society. The need for such laws is usually highlighted by current demands in the society they serve, but by the time they take effect those demands may have already changed, with the result that the law is static and often out of place.

It is not strange, therefore, that there are already *two schools of thought among canonists.* Some are already calling for a review of the Code because they believe that in its present form it lacks or simply ignores a lot of fundamental issues that affect the accomplishment of the salvific mission of the Church. Others have simply lost hope and do not believe that the Code can be improved to satisfy the aspirations the people of God had when Pope John XXIII first announced his intention to reform the Code of Canon Law.

It is too early to reform or review the 1983 Code. One of the few possibilities that can help to accommodate the need for the Code to become an instrument of development in the Church is for Church tribunals at different levels to give wider interpretations to the provisions of the Code. Such interpretation should reflect the environment in which the faithful live. Eventually the particular churches will have to play a more active role in matters and cultures which in themselves are peculiar and particular, but which do not challenge the basic principles of Catholicism.

José Dammert Bellido

The New Code in an Andean Diocese

DIOCESES FAR from the European canonical movement can find *perspectives in the new legislation to help them in their pastoral work*. It has gathered together those dispensations and exemptions granted by Rome the constant application of which had led to their being extended generally throughout the Latin Church. The idea of the Church as people of God, the presentation of the Christian faithful as active members of the Church and the inclusion of the rights and duties of the laity, which were ignored in the 1917 Code, are all useful and positive for pastoral work in the Andean environment.

On the other hand, *certain limitations* and the desire to standardise diocesan administration to a universal system make some of the new provisions impracticable in dioceses which cover a wide area and large population, but which are short of personnel and resources.

I

'*The relaxation of a merely ecclesiastical law*' contemplated in canon 85 is much more flexible than previous legislation on dispensations, in that it recognises that this faculty belongs to the 'ordinary and immediate power' of the bishop and its exercise is required by his pastoral function (can. 381), whereas reservation of judgment by the pope is exceptional and is confined to certain matters or cases for the good of the whole Church. This innovation will make the pastoral mission of Third World bishops considerably easier.

The effort to *adapt the common legislation to regional situations* is another sign of the new spirit informing the new Code. In some cases, ruling on particular norms for their region or country is left to the judgment of bishops' conferences. Here are some random examples: the rite of marriage is to be 'in keeping with those customs of place and people which accord with the Christian spirit' (can. 1120); the training of priests is to be in accordance with the 'pastoral needs of each region or province' (can. 242 par. 1) etc. The increased recognition of civil laws (22) expresses the same desire to make universal norms apply more flexibly. The reduction of the penal code also makes it easier to put it into practice (the current Book VI contains 88 canons as compared with 219 in the previous one). All this depends for its application on the creative strength of the bishops; they must have the boldness recommended by Pope Paul VI and not be afraid of possible risks or fall into narrow scruples.

Likewise some norms are to be extended to *unforeseen cases*, which are similar to those in the statutes, e.g. canon 792, which anticipates assistance to workers and students coming from mission contries—and in the Third World migrants from rural areas must also be taken into consideration.

The relations between the *Apostolic Nuncios and the bishops' conferences* will be based on close collaboration 'without detriment to the legitimate power of the latter' (can. 364 nos. 2 and 3; can. 365 par. 2). This has altered previous legislation which provided for surveillance (can. 267), and the new relationship will allow for an efficient collaboration making use of the wisdom and experience of the pope's representative for the development of pastoral work at national and diocesan level. Such collaboration looks to the present and the future and there are examples of it in action in the nuncios Lombardi in Brazil, Arrigoni in Peru and Bertoli in Colombia, who were supported and encouraged by the substitute of the Secretariat of State Giovanni B. Montini, who has to proclaim the principles of the Code from the papal throne.

Another positive provision of the Code is collaboration between bishops and religious orders (can. 678 *ff*); on the other hand the diocesan bishop is to do all he can to encourage vocations to the various ministries and the religious life (can. 385).

The establishment of *interdiocesan tribunals* (canons 1423 and 1439) will help the administration of justice in countries where there is a severe shortage of personnel.

II

Of vital importance to the development of pastoral work in an Andean diocese is the recognition of the *role of the laity* in the spreading of the divine message of salvation to all human beings all over the world (can. 225 par. 1).

Throughout the Code there is legislation for this *lay mission*, or situations are recognised which would make it easier to put into practice. The fixing of the age of majority at eighteen (can. 97 par. 1) is useful in a continent with a predominantly young population, where workers begin work very young, even in childhood, and also marry early.

The option for the poor and the young made by the Puebla bishops' conference, fits in with the poverty which forces children to work, so that opting for the young is opting for the poor and vice versa.

The special interest priests and diocesan bishops must take in mature vocations to the sacred ministries (can. 233 par. 2) is also a recognition of the particular situation in this so-called New World.

The requirement pointed out to Christians to 'promote social justice, and, remembering the Lord's command, help the poor with our own goods' (can. 22 par. 2 and can. 747 par. 2) and to religious houses 'to avoid any appearance of immoderate luxury and accumulation of goods' (can. 634 par. 2) suggests its immediate application in a country submerged in poverty.

The urging of the laity to 'impregnate and perfect the temporal order with the gospel spirit and thus bear witness to Christ' (canons 225 par. 2 and 327) illuminates the *social and political action of Christians* in situations of great delicacy and urgency. However, lay activity is not confined to a mission in the world, they also have an important role to play within the Church (275 par. 2).

Within the Church, *lay activity has been extended*, including activity by lay brothers and sisters. Canon 129 par. 2 declares that 'in the exercise of the power of government the lay faithful can co-operate in accordance with their rights', although the verb 'co-operate' is fairly ambiguous. Canon 228 par. 1 states that 'they have the capacity to be called to those ecclesiatical offices and duties which they can fulfil according to the prescriptions of the law'. Among these offices, they can: be judges (can. 1421 par. 2), ecclesiastical administrators and members of the diocesan or parochial financial council (canons 492 and 537), chancellor and notary (canons 482-3), assessors and auditors, promoter of justice and defender of the bond (in matrimonial cases). (Canons 1424, 1428 par. 2, 1435); be members of the diocesan or parochial pastoral council (canons 511 and 536); take part in the diocesan synod (can. 463 par. 1

n. 5) or be invited (par. 2), to particular councils (can. 443 par. 4); they can also obtain academic degrees and receive authority to teach sacred sciences (can. 229 par. 2 and 3).

The term used includes both men and women. For dioceses short of personnel these provisions will be of help in judicial, curial and financial administration and also in teaching, always supposing that those appointed are distinguished 'by their knowledge, wisdom and integrity' (canons 228 par. 2 and 231 par. 1) and are given full confidence. Very important is the authority that can be given by the diocesan bishop to persons 'who do not have the priestly character' to be in charge of a parish (can. 512 par. 2). Because Third World dioceses may cover such a vast areas and their parishes be so large, this permission to empower religious or lay people who are not priests to look after a parish will extend pastoral care to many parishioners who live far away from parochial centres. This grants lay Christians various powers to exercise the Church's funciton of teaching and sanctification (can. 230 par. 30).

These functions are specified in other canons as the ministry of the Word (canons 759 and 766), cathechesis (canons 780 and 785); lay missions (can. 784). As to liturgical functions (can. 835 par. 4): the ministries of reader and acolyte (albeit reserved to men) (can. 230 par. 1); reader, commentator, singer and others in liturgical ceremonies (can. 230 par. 2); presiding over liturgical prayers (canons 12–48 par. 2); administering baptism (can. 861 par. 2) and Holy Communion (can. 910 par. 2), also the last rites (can. 911 par. 2); helping a blind or sick priest celebrate mass (can. 930 par. 2); exposition and reservation of the Blessed Sacrament (can. 943); assisting officially at weddings (can. 1112); administering sacramentals (can. 1168).

The concession to administer baptism comes from an oral favour granted by Paul VI for the benefit of the peasants of the Cajamarca diocese, which was later extended to the whole of Peru and included in the present Code, because it was working well. General absolution, authorised by canon 961 par. 2 n. 2, with the relative prescriptions, is very useful in this region of the Andes, because of the scarcity of confessors, as it means that the faithful can receive other sacraments in the grace of God.

III

In other ways the *new Code remains very European and urban, particularly in the regulation of the diocesan curia* (can. 469), which is complicated or ecclesiastical jurisdictions with reduced personnel. There is a danger of getting bogged down in petty bureacratic rules to the detriment of pastoral work. The

Roman ministries, the organisms of CELAM and even the National Episcopal Conference flood the dioceses with documents, inquiries, consultations, projects, outlines etc. which do not correspond to the reality, or only minimally. Or they set up campaigns with their corresponding propaganda with detailed aims, which reduce the diocesan curias to a merely executive role. In curias which are poor in personnel and resources, in which the bishop and chancellor as well as fulfilling their own functions, take part in parish and chaplaincy work, teaching and confessions, as well as having national or even continental responsibilities, an attempt to keep in line with the rulings of superior authorities becomes an intolerable burden, unless a large freedom of spirit prevails.

Of course entities like the episcopal council (can. 473), or the various general and episcopal vicariates (can. 475) are reserved to large dioceses, but it is necessary to lower certain standards to be more in keeping with our reality. The requirement of a minimum number of six members for the College of diocesan consultors (can. 502 par. 1) is high for dioceses and prelacies, so that it has been found necessary to ask permission to reduce it to four. I think this situation should have been thought of, so that it would not have been necessary to have special recourse to the Holy See in every case. Formerly bishops of the Indies enjoyed privileges and special permissions; in 1899 Pope Leo XIII granted trentennial faculties on the occasion of the Plenary Latin American Council. When these expired they were renewed every ten years until Vatican II, which accepted many of them. Other privileges were granted by Propaganda Fide to mission lands. I think that *circumstance still exist today requiring legislation differing from the common law.*

The abundance of titles for diocesan bishops (cardinal archbishop, primate, archbishop, apostolic vicar, prelate, diocesan administrator with powers of a residential bishop) causes confusion among the faithful and civil functionaries, who understand neither the sameness nor the differences in these funcitons. A people without medieval traditions, because they have not lived with them, and who for centuries only heard speak of an archbishop and a number of bishops, gets lost among so many names, or believes that it is like a military hierarchy with ranks like the army. *Simplification* would produce a clearer and simpler vision of the pastors of the Church.

The persistence of *provincial councils* with all the solemnity and conditions surrounding them (can. 439), as compared with the greater flexibility of episcopal conferences, becomes inoperable for ecclesiastical provinces (can. 431) with three to four bishops.

An institution which needs restructuring is the *visit 'ad limina apostolorum'* (can. 400). A personal audience with the Holy Father lasting about ten minutes, which is understandable in view of the large number of bishops to be received, is too short to go into the pastoral problems of each diocese and the country. The collective audience must change its form. Instead of greetings and response, which could be sent by letter, what is needed is a working session lasting at least two hours, with questions, replies and commentaries. This is done to some extent during the pleasant informal conversation at lunch, but not nearly enough.

The visit to the dicasteries (departments) of the Roman curia sometimes produces the impression of mere formality and nothing can be gone into at any depth. Here too a much longer conversation, both collective and individual, is required. The sending of the five-yearly report should lead the officials of the dicasteries to ask personally for verbal explanations, not just to their writing back a few months later with no possibility of dialogue. Of course the curial officials have many duties, but travelling to far away places at great expense, for the sake of protocol and nothing more, is wasteful and unsatis-factory.

IV

The cathedral chapters, with four prebendaries, supported by very small stipends from the Peruvian government (at present each member of the chapter receives ten US dollars a month) are destined to disappear for lack of money. It is a very difficult and serious pastoral problem to apply canonical rules in large areas with valleys and mountains between two and four thousand metres above sea level, and roads whose distances are measured in hours not kilometres, or in heavily populated areas with one or two priests. These circumstances make worthy and pious prescriptions on the rights and duties of parish priests go up in smoke (canons 528 to 530). Of course it is possible to try to keep the spirit of these dispositions but one feels it slipping away. When the bishop pays a *pastoral visit* (canons 396–8) he finds himself in a situation of gazing compassionately at the crowd, being unable to apply the legislation at all closely, merely telling people to 'do what they can', while sometimes correcting some scandalous abuse.

The *parochial system* laid out by the Code does not correspond to the Andean reality. It should be remembered that a diocese covering an area of 15,000 square kilometres and half a million inhabitants, has twenty-six parishes, about ten of which are vacant. Either the parish priest attends to the urban population living in the parish capital, doing for them what is laid down in the Code, but completely neglecting the people living in outlying villages or scattered over the countryside. Or he can embark on a rural missionary programme, only to receive complaints from the town dwellers that they have no priest to look after them.

He can either be a *parish priest or an itinerant rural missionary* to educate, guide and encourage the base communities and teams of catechists and give peasants the sacraments. This situation requires careful study to extend, support and encourage pastoral work in these huge rural areas, which are being penetrated by sects because they are not properly looked after by Catholics. Continental and world meetings study the pastoral problems of the great cities, a recent phenomenon, but pastoral work in rural areas is neglected.

Undoubtedly the concessions granted to the laity mentioned above make the work of the parish easier, but a few aspects are still left out, like for example the *anointing of the sick*, which is specially reserved to the parish priest (can. 530 n. 3) or a priest (can. 1003 par. 2 and 3); in practice this makes it a non-existent sacrament in the Andes, where the peasants demand 'signs and means by which to express and strengthen their faith, give service to God and increase human holiness' (can. 840); they do not just want the commendation of their souls.

The requirement that each parish should keep a *record of deaths* (can. 535 par. 1), which used to be limited to those which occurred in the parish church or immediate neighbourhood, is unreasonable, and anyway there are now civil records. The existence in each civil province of only two or three parishes, sometimes attended by just one priest make it impracticable to have an archpriest, deacon or outside vicar (canons 553 to 555).

In order to take care of the innumerable requests for the celebrations of masses, the custom has been introduced of *celebrating masses for shared intentions*, that is to say every petitioner brings his or her own particular intention and gives a voluntary offering. Sometimes there are ten or fifteen intentions, which according to canon 948 require the celebration of that number of masses, which would be impossible. In the Cathedral of Cajamarca, the total collected from one day to another during the month corresponds to the stipends that would be obtained from the celebration of thirty masses, by which the disposition of canon 947 is fulfilled. Those bringing offerings are satisfied by hearing their petitions mentioned in the prayer of the faithful or in the respective place in the Canon. It is a particular solution to a restrictive disposition of the common law.

V

In spite of its consideration of the role of the laity the Code still has an *excessively intraecclesial and hierarchical view*, and leaves out or includes merely incidentally subjects which should have been considered in their own right. Care of teachers who teach religion in non-Catholic schools figures as an irregularity within the Catholic school system (can. 804 par. 2); pastoral care of students at non-Catholic universities appears under the heading of Catholic universities, almost in passing (can. 813), as does the teaching of theological disciplines 'in any institution of higher studies' (can. 812). Scientific collaboration between universities comes under the heading of ecclesiastical universities and faculties (can. 820). The scientific rigour required in Catholic schools must be extended to other universities (can. 800 par. 2). In areas which have no Catholic schools or universities, pastoral work in lay institutions needs special care. This is also the case in other dioceses because of the large numbers of Catholic students and teachers in State institutions. In Peru 93 per cent attend State institutions and only 6 per cent Catholic ones.

Contributors

JOSE DAMMERT BELLIDO was born in Lima (Peru) in 1917. He gained a doctorate in jurisprudence in Pavia (Italy) in 1937. He taught Roman and ecclesiastical law in the Catholic University of Peru. He has been bishop of Cajamarca since 1962. He is consultor of the Pontifical Commision *'pro recognoscendo C.J.C.'*, and vice-president of the Peru Episcopal Conference. He has written a number of juridical and historical articles in European and Peruvian journals, books on the history of Cajamarca, and *Veinticinco anos al servicio de la Iglesia-Seleccion de textos y Testimonios* (1983).

JEAN BERNHARD was born at Ribeauvillé, France, in 1914 and was ordained a priest in 1938. He studied at Strasbourg, Rome, the Ecole des Hautes Etudes, and the law faculty of the University of Paris. He is a doctor of theology and of canon law (Strasbourg), and holds the diploma of higher legal studies (Paris). He was a professor in the Strasbourg theological faculty from 1958 to 1982, and director of the Institute of Canon Law from 1970 to 1982. In 1951 he founded the *Revue de Droit canonique* which he still directs. He has been *officialis* of the diocese of Strasbourg since 1952 and worked with the Pontifical Commission for the revision of the Code of Canon Law. He is a member of the French Committee of Canon Law. He has published the two-volume collection (Cod. Vat. lat. 3832): *La Forme primitive de la collection en deux livres, source de la collection en 74 titres et de la collection d'Anselme de Lucques.* He has contributed to several symposia and to a number of periodicals on canon law. Most of his articles on marital law were published in the *Revue de Droit canonique*.

STEVEN BWANA was born in 1949 at Musoma, Tanzania. He gained the degrees of Bachelor of Laws and Master of Laws (in criminology and penology) at the University of Dar es Salaam and his doctorate *in utroque iure* at the university of the Lateran, Rome, in 1982. At present he is working as Training and Research Officer at the Court of Appeal of Tanzania, Dar es Salaam. He is a member of the National Team of Catholic Professionals of Tanzania. He was at one time a member of the Executive Commission of Caritas International.

EUGENIO CORECCO was born in Airolo in Switzerland in 1931 and ordained in 1955. He holds a doctorate from the Catholic University of Milan and lectures in canon law at the University of Fribourg. He has published a number of articles on aspects of the new Code of Canon Law: 'I presupposti culturali ed ecclesiologici del nuovo "Codex"', 'Sacerdocio e Presbiterio nel CIC', 'Natura e struttura della "sacra potestas" nella dottrina e nel nuovo CIC', 'I laici nel nuovo CIC', 'Il catologo dei doveri-diritti nel CIC', 'Theological Justification of the Codification of the Latin Canon Law' (Acts of the Vth International Congress of Canon Law, Ottawa 1984).

JOHN FARIS, a priest of the Maronite Church, was born in 1951 in Pennsylvania. He was ordained a priest in 1976 for the Diocese of Saint Maron-U.S.A. In 1980, he gained a doctorate in Eastern Canon Law from the Pontifical Institute of Oriental Studies (Rome). He currently serves as Chancellor of the Diocese of Saint Maron and Lecturer at The Catholic University of America. He has published various articles on Eastern canon law and interecclesial issues.

LIBERO GEROSA was born in Stabio in Switzerland in 1949, and graduated in theology at the University of Fribourg in 1974. He was ordained priest in the diocese of Lugano the following year. After some years of pastoral work with young people he was appointed university chaplain and is now 'Studies Counsellor' at the theological faculty at Fribourg. He obtained his doctorate in theology in 1984 with his thesis examining whether excommunication is a punishment. He has published articles in various theological and canonical reviews.

RICHARD HILL, S.J., was born in Los Angeles, California, in 1928 and ordained in 1958. He received the licentiate in sacred theology from Alma College, Los Gatos, California, in 1959 and the doctorate in canon law from the Gregorian University in 1963. He has been a professor of canon law since then at the Jesuit School of Theology at Berkeley, California. He has published articles on religious in *The Jurist* and *Review for Religious* and commented on canons 124–203 in *The Code of Canon Law: A Text and Commentary* (1985) and on canons 673–683, 'Apostolate of Religious Institutes' in *Religious Institutes, Secular Institutes, Societies of the Apostolic Life: A Handbook on Canons 573–746* (1985).

JOHN HUELS, O.S.M., was born in St. Louis in 1950. Ordained a priest of the Servite Order in 1976, he served in a parish for three years before earning a doctorate in canon law at the Catholic University of America. Since 1982 he has taught canon law at Catholic Theological Union in Chicago. His publications include *The Faithful of Christ: The New Canon Law for the Laity* (1983) and *The New Pastoral Companion: A Canon Law Handbook for Catholic Ministry* (1986), both published by Franciscan Herald Press of Chicago. He has contributed numerous articles to canonical, liturgical, and pastoral journals, and has authored the section on the Eucharist in *The Code of Canon Law: A Text and Commentary* (1985) which was commissioned by the Canon Law Society of America.

PETER HUIZING, S.J., born at Haarlem, Netherlands in 1911, entered the Society of Jesus in 1931 and was ordained to the priesthood in 1941. He studied at the universities of Amsterdam, Nijmegen, Louvain and the Gregorian, and is a licentiate of both philosophy and theology, a master of laws and a doctor of canon law. He is emeritus professor of canon law at Nijmegen. He was a consultor of the pontifical commission for the revision of the Code of Canon Law. Among his publications are: *Schema structurae iuris canonici matrimonialis* (1963); *De Trentse huwelijksvorm* (1966); *Um eine neue Kirchenordnung*, in Müller/Elsener/Huizing *Vom Kirchenrecht zur Kirchenordnung?*; and various articles in *Concilium, Periodica, Gregorianum, The Jurist*, etc.

ELIZABETH MCDONOUGH, O.P. entered the Dominican Sisters of Columbus, Ohio in 1963 and pursued studies at Ohio Dominican College, Fairfield University, and The Catholic University of America. She earned her doctorate in canon law from CUA in 1982 and is currently assistant professor of canon law at Catholic University. She has taught canon law at the Pontifical College Josephinum (Columbus, Ohio), has lectured widely in the United States on the topic of canon law for religious, and is canonical consultant for several religious congregations. Her publications include *Religious in the 1983 Code: New Approaches to the New Law,* 'Departure and Dismissal' in *A Handbook for Religious*, 'Reflections of a Canon Lawyer' in *Religious Life in the U.S. Church: The New Dialogue*, as well as contributions to *CLSA Proceedings, The Jurist, Spirituality Today*, and *The Way Supplement*.

FRANCIS MORRISEY, O.M.I. was born in Charlottetown, P.E.I., Canada in 1936, and ordained to the priesthood (Oblates of Mary Immaculate) in 1961. He studied at the University of Ottawa and Saint Paul University, gaining licentiates in philosophy and theology, a master's degree in religious education and a doctorate in canon law. He was dean of the Faculty of Canon Law, Saint Paul University, Ottawa, between 1972–1984. Presently he is professor of canon law in the same faculty. He is past president of the Canadian Canon Law Society. He is author of numerous articles in various periodicals, particularly in the areas of canon law and Canadian church history. He is honorary life member of the Canon Law Societies of America, Canada, Great Britain and Ireland, Australia and New Zealand.

RICHARD POTZ studied law in Vienna, Rome, Constantinople and Selonika, and has been professor of canon law at the Faculty of Jurisprudence in Vienna since 1981. A member of the Vienna Catholic Academy, he is particularly concerned with the canon law of the Eastern churches. His publications include: *Patriarch und Synode in Konstantinopel* (1971) and *Die Geltung kirchenrechtlicher Normen* (1978).

ALBERT STEIN was born in 1925. He is an executive council member of the Baden State Evangelical Church and an honorary professor of practical theology and canon law at the University of Heidelberg. His particular field of research is canon law as it relates to ministry, marriage and ecumenism. His publications include *Probleme evangelischer Lehrbeanstandung* (1967), *Evangelische Laienpredigt* (1972), *Evangelisches Kirchenrecht, ein Lernbuch* (1980, 1985).

CONCILIUM

CONCILIUM

CONCILIUM 1985

All back issues are still in print: available from bookshops (price £3.95) or direct from the publisher (£4.45/US$7.70/Can$8.70 including postage and packing).

T. & T. CLARK LTD, 59 GEORGE STREET, EDINBURGH EH2 2LQ, SCOTLAND

Holy Trinity Church
Marylebone Road
London NW1 4DU

The Country Parish
Anthony Russell

As the nature of the countryside changes, so does the role of the parish priest. In a careful and thorough analysis of both the historical evidence and future trends, Anthony Russell offers suggestions for an effective country ministry, despite the financial and other constraints which have led to a contraction in the rural parochial system.

Publication July 17th   **£9.50**

The Christian Priest Today
Michael Ramsey

Michael Ramsey's book of charges to ordination candidates has long been a classic of its kind and has provided inspiration not just for those who are in the ordained ministry but for many others who minister. This new edition has been expanded to consider the nature of vocation today and the changes in the priesthood.

'What a privilege it must have been to receive these charges in the flesh, and to hear the voice and catch the chuckle and watch the eyebrows in operation. Having the book is the next best thing.' *Richard Holloway*   **£3.95**

The Clerical Profession
Anthony Russell

This thought provoking and thoroughly researched book shows how the role of the Church of England clergyman changed with the industrialization of society and a consequent need for professionalism. Dr Russell makes his own contribution to the current debate about the nature of the ministry of the Church of England by considering the forms which this may have to assume in the future.

'This is an excellent book which should stimulate thought and provide abundant material for discussion groups.' *Church of England Newspaper*

£7.50

The Priestlike Task
Wesley Carr

The role of the priesthood within society at large is undergoing re-evaluation. Wesley Carr considers the position of the priest within his environment and suggests ways in which the effectiveness of his ministry can be increased.

£3.95

Paid to Care?
Alastair V Campbell

Is it possible to talk of 'expertise' in Christian love? Alastair Campbell looks at the limits of professionalism and shows how a Christian perception of caring is essential within the professional relationship.

£3.95

Available from SPCK and other good bookshops.